Entrepreneurship in the Global Firm

SAGE STRATEGY SERIES

The objective of the *Sage Strategy Series* is to publish significant contributions to the field of management in general, and strategy in particular, with a special emphasis on young and rising authors. The books aim to make a scholarly and provocative contribution to the field of strategy, and will be of a high intellectual standard, containing new empirical or new theoretical contributions. We are especially interested in books that provide new insights into existing ideas as well as those that challenge conventional thinking by linking together levels of analysis which were traditionally distinct. We expect to receive some contributions from scholars in departments outside of strategy, such as accounting, where the theme is of relevance to strategy.

A special feature of the series is the active advisory board of strategy scholars from leading, international business schools in Europe, USA and the Far East. They are endorsing the series in much the same way as the editorial board of leading journals such as the *Strategic Management Journal* endorses its articles. We believe that the contribution of the Sage brand name and that of an active and strong board will be a unique selling point for book buyers, and other academics.

Entrepreneurship in the Global Firm

Julian Birkinshaw

SAGE Publications
London • Thousand Oaks • New Delhi

First published 2000

SAGE Publications Ltd
6 Bonhill Street
London EC2A 4PU

SAGE Publications Inc
2455 Teller Road
Thousand Oaks, California 91320

SAGE Publications India Pvt Ltd
32, M-Block Market
Greater Kailash – I
New Delhi 110 048

British Library Cataloguing in Publication data

A catalogue record for this book is available from
the British Library

ISBN 0 7619 5809 6
ISBN 0 7619 5808 8 (pbk)

Library of Congress catalog card number 00 131447

Typeset by Photoprint, Torquay
Printed in Great Britain by the Cromwell Press Ltd,
Trowbridge, Wiltshire

To Laura, for her enthusiasm and support during this long project

Contents

List of Figures

List of Tables

Foreword

The key theme of Julian Birkinshaw's exciting book is that the manager of the subsidiary of the multinational enterprise is now a relevant unit of analysis. The large MNCs he has studied have average sales in excess of US$ 20 billion and operate a dispersed network of foreign subsidiaries in 50 or more countries. The managers of these subsidiaries are now decision makers (taking 'subsidiary iniatives') within interorganizational networks. The head office managers are also network participants but can no longer operate as hierarchical controllers.

A major contribution of Julian Birkinshaw's careful empirical and theoretical research is to broaden this principle of subsidiary initiatives from its origins in the behavioural analysis of subsidiary managers in smaller countries such as Canada and Sweden to all managers in dispersed multinational networks, including those that are 'triad-based' (in the US, EU and Japan). His perspective is that of a subsidiary manager operating in a network, and in its extreme version this means that all managers are subsidiary managers. This presents challenges for both managers and policy makers who still view multinationals as hierarchies.

In this book, which is charaterized by exceptional clarity of thought and writing, Julian Birkinshaw stakes out ground as a major new thinker in the fields of international business and strategic management. Students and scholars in these fields will find this a challenging and rewarding book which pushes back the frontiers of knowledge in a significant manner.

Alan M. Rugman
Templeton College, University of Oxford

Preface

There appear to be two traditional approaches to writing what I would call 'academic' books in management studies. One approach is to base the book on a single line of research that the author(s) have been pursuing for a number of years. Often these books emerge from doctoral theses – they are well argued, strong both theoretically and empirically, and they address very well delineated research questions. At the same time they are typically somewhat narrow and – more importantly – rather inaccessible to anyone who has not spent some time immersed in the debates and ideas of that particular subfield.

At the other extreme there are many books that are either texts for masters or doctoral programmes, or 'review' books that seek to present a synopsis of an entire field of research. Gareth Morgan's *Images of Organizations* (1986) represents a classic in this genre, in that it provides a very broad coverage of literature, organizes it in a creative and thought-provoking way *and* is written in an accessible manner that makes it appropriate for students as well as established academics. By virtue of their breadth, however, such books are inappropriate vehicles for presenting the results of the authors' own research.

The current book attempts to span these two traditions. In content, it falls clearly into the first category – the research is drawn from my doctoral thesis and from a number of studies that I undertook in subsequent years, and it addresses a number of rather narrowly defined research questions. In its style, however, the book aspires to membership of the second category. I have pitched the research issues in much broader terms than the data can actually address. I have also brought in examples and research findings from other studies, in order to provide the reader with a relatively comprehensive perspective on the issues covered. Finally, I have also chosen to write in what should be a reasonably accessible style. My target audience, if such a group can be defined, might be individuals just embarking on their doctoral studies. I assume little or no knowledge of the prevailing theories, and I have deliberately presented my research in qualitative and anecdotal form rather than presenting the empirical material in its entirety.

Consistent with the schizophrenic approach described above, the book has two objectives. First, I am attempting to integrate and present in a single volume the line of research that began in 1992 while I was a doctoral student at the University of Western Ontario and continued until

1999, through a short spell at the University of Strathclyde, a four-year appointment at the Stockholm School of Economics and into the beginning of my employment at the London Business School. Many of the chapters in this book are built on papers that have been published elsewhere, and other parts are drawn from my unpublished doctoral dissertation. But from my current vantage point, it seems clear that there are underlying themes to all of my work in the last seven years that probably cannot be gleaned from any one of the contributory papers. This book represents an attempt to draw out those themes and to place them in their wider context.

My second objective is to attempt to shed light on *the role of the subsidiary manager* in a multinational corporation. At first glance the subsidiary manager's role is straightforward – the president of 3M Sweden, for example, is responsible for all 3M's operations in Sweden – but when one digs deeper a much more ambiguous and complex picture emerges. For instance, is the subsidiary manager acting in the interests of the parent company, the subsidiary itself or the country of operation? What factors shape his or her behaviour on a day-to-day basis? And what are the trade-offs, conscious and otherwise, underlying his or her long-term objectives? None of these questions are new or unresearched *per se*, but as I moved deeper into this line of research it became clear that most literature on multinational corporations has been written – implicitly at least – from the perspective of the parent company managers. Such a perspective sees foreign subsidiaries as instruments of their parent company, whose behaviours *should* be aligned with the strategic imperatives of the corporation as a whole. Even leading writers such as Chris Bartlett, Sumantra Ghoshal and Gunnar Hedlund acknowledge the importance of innovative and entrepreneurial endeavours at the level of the foreign subsidiary, but with a normative bias that such endeavours be structured and controlled by head office managers.

Because my research up to now has been conducted primarily at the level of the foreign subsidiary, I find myself championing the subsidiary's cause in a way that to some extent pushes against the writings of the leading scholars in the field. I see subsidiary managers sitting in a unique position where they have considerable *de facto* discretion to act as they see fit. This sometimes means pursuing activities that have not been mandated by head office managers, and sometimes even deliberately acting against the expressed wishes of managers in the parent company. Empirically, I know this to be the case. However, unlike many others I do not necessarily see such 'subversive' behaviour as an evil that should be stamped out. Rather it depends a lot on the specific challenges and opportunities that the subsidiary manager is facing.

The dilemma, in a nutshell, is that existing theory does not adequately capture the real-world challenges faced by the manager of a foreign subsidiary. I do not want to be seen as the proponent of a corporate anarchy in which every subsidiary manager does as he or she sees fit, but at the same time I have seen enough cases of success stories that began as subversion that I cannot buy into traditional agency theory models. This, then, is my second objective in the current book: *to make sense of the role of the subsidiary manager from the perspective of that manager.* In doing this, the book inevitably strays into more applied territory because it documents the issues as they appear to subsidiary managers. The challenge, which I can only claim partial success in meeting, is to reconcile these observed behaviours and predispositions with the various theoretical perspectives that are traditionally used in studying multi-national corporations.

I would like to anticipate one possible criticism of this book, namely my expressed intention to speak in general terms about multinational management, but then to focus primarily on my own research. Surely, the reader will think, there must be other equally-good studies that shed light on these issues. Indeed there are – I realize that my own studies make up a small fraction of the research in this area, and consequently it seems in some ways a little odd that I would focus only on my own. My approach guards against such a criticism in two ways. First, I am offering a perspective on the world, which involves presenting a stream of research in such a way that it informs that perspective. Other perspectives will be mentioned, and in some cases will be discussed in detail. Second, I am careful to draw from and reference the work of other scholars whose approaches or findings are complementary to my own. Inevitably there will be some research that is neglected, but I believe that readers will find a discussion of all the 'major' works that – according to conventional wisdom – exist in this field.

While a list of mentors, collaborators and influences can never be complete, the relatively short length of my academic career so far makes it easy to list the principal individuals who should be acknowledged in this book. The Richard Ivey School of Business (formerly Western Business School) was my academic home for four years, and was an excellent place to start my career. Professors Nick Fry, Rod White, Paul Beamish, Peter Killing and many others steered me through my coursework and towards an interesting and challenging thesis topic. My doctoral colleagues, who have all moved on to academic careers around the world, were also very influential: Martha Maznevski, Andrew Inkpen, Carl Fey, Derrick Neufeld, Danny Szpiro, Paul Kedrosky and Detlev Nitsch, to name just a few of them. Alan Rugman at the University of Toronto (now at Oxford University) was also an important source of inspiration in this period, and it was his initiative that led to this book being written in the first place.

At the University of Strathclyde I formed a very important relationship with Professor Neil Hood, who has experience in this area as a manager, a public policy maker and a neutral academic observer. Neil and I have coauthored several papers, and our collaborative endeavours will, I am sure, continue. I would also like to thank Steve Young and Ewen Peters for their feedback on my ideas during my time in Glasgow.

The Institute of International Business at the Stockholm School of Economics was my home for almost four years, and is probably the best place in the world to do this sort of research. Gunnar Hedlund was a major influence on me from the early days of my career, and was responsible for luring me to Stockholm. During those four years I also benefited enormously from the intellectual insights of my colleagues: Udo Zander, Jonas Ridderstråle, Kjell Nordström, Örjan Sölvell, Peter Hagström and many others.

My current place of work is the London Business School, and while this book was essentially written before I arrived there, it is still important to thank Sumantra Ghoshal for the feedback and advice he has given me over the years. While this book represents the end of a major chapter in my research career, my interest in the inner workings of the multinational corporation continues. Sumantra, John Stopford, Costas Markides and many of my other current colleagues are already providing me with stimuli for further and deeper research in this area. To these individuals, and many others unnamed, I offer my heartfelt thanks.

Finally, I would like to thank Rosemary Nixon at Sage for her encouragement, editorial comments and ideas about how this book should be positioned. I have gone through several rounds of major changes in putting the book together, and the fact that each round has resulted in a substantially better product is testament to Rosemary's skill as an editor.

1

Introduction and Overview

The departure point of this book will be familiar to anyone even moderately versed in the management literature: that the world of business is becoming ever more global in scope, and consequently that large global firms (hereafter referred to as MNCs, multinational corporations) are emerging as some of the most influential and powerful institutions in the global economy, transcending and possibly even displacing nation states in their ability to drive economic development.

Such a bold statement would often be backed up with pages of analysis, explaining and justifying that business is indeed becoming more global, and making a case that somehow the rules of the game are changing in a way that demands new strategic and/or organizational responses from MNCs. But the approach here is somewhat different. While many of the changes alluded to above are clearly under way, this book has a very different story to tell, one which does not even require the world of business to be changing in fundamental ways. The story is one of *internally driven changes to the strategy and structure of the multinational corporation*.

The book draws on research conducted by the author and many others into the workings of large MNCs – corporations such as Ericsson, GE, BP and Nestlé, whose annual sales revenues typically exceed $20 billion and whose operations span 50 or more countries. It is concerned with understanding what the concept of strategy means for such large and geographically dispersed corporations, and how they can be structured in such a way that they can reap the benefits of size without sacrificing the benefits of local presence. This is certainly not a new research agenda – pioneers such as John Fayerweather (1969), John Stopford and Louis Wells (1972) and C.K. Prahalad (1975) addressed these issues more than twenty years ago, and there has been a steady stream of research ever since. But one common theme that is often not explicitly recognized is that all the leading studies in this area are written from the perspective of head office managers, the individuals at the corporate centre. The focus on these executives is of course of the utmost importance – they are accountable for the performance of their corporation, and they have formal authority to enforce whatever changes they deem appropriate. But if we believe some of the recent advances that portray the MNC as an interorganizational network (Ghoshal and Bartlett, 1990) or a nearly recomposable system (Hedlund, 1997), it becomes increasingly obvious that head office managers have a less firm grip on the worldwide activities of their corporation than they would like. Stories of foreign subsidiaries deliberately going against the directives of their parent company, and even severing their formal ties with the corporation, are commonplace. And the development of sophisticated socialization mechanisms – such as the use of expatriate managers and global training programmes – is frequently discussed as a means of mitigating the limitations of more traditional control mechanisms.

The unique positioning of this book, then, is its focus on the foreign-owned subsidiary as the principal unit of analysis. Certainly there have been plenty of other studies of subsidiaries over the last twenty years, but they have typically embraced the conventional line of thinking that the subsidiary 'does what it is told' by the parent company. The approach taken here, by contrast, is to view subsidiary managers as more or less 'free agents'. They are employed by the multinational parent company and they take actions that they believe are in the best interests of the corporation as a whole, but that does not mean they will always act in conformance with the expressed wishes of head office managers. Such subversive behaviour may sound like a good way of cutting short a promising career, but the fact of the matter is that there is plentiful evidence that it occurs, and that it *can* be extremely beneficial to both subsidiary and parent. One of the intriguing dilemmas that comes out in several places in the book is the split personality that effective subsidiary managers appear to have – they are both good corporate citizens and mavericks at the same time.

But it is not just the 'free agent' perspective on the subsidiary manager that makes this book important. It is the observation that the actions of subsidiary managers can have widespread implications for both the structure and the strategy of the multinational corporation as a whole. The research described in the book began with a few simple accounts of maverick subsidiary managers and the initiatives they had pursued, but in following their stories, and the consequences that their actions had elsewhere, it becomes apparent that the research has important implications at the level of the corporation, as well as at the level of the subsidiary. To return to an earlier point, the MNC is much better viewed as an interorganizational network than a monolithic hierarchy, because every node in that network (that is, each subsidiary) has the potential to take actions that can influence the rest of the network. Clearly, parent company managers are still the most influential actors in the network, and the best positioned to drive strategic or structural changes in response to changes in the business environment. But one cannot ignore the fact that many of the strategic and structural changes that are observed in MNCs are internally driven, that is, initiated from below by subsidiary managers.

What sort of strategic and structural changes are we talking about? One example will be mentioned here – the tendency of large MNCs to locate more and more value-adding activities outside the home country. The traditional model, as exemplified by corporations such as Caterpillar Tractor and Matsushita, was of a strong corporate centre in which all technological development, most manufacturing and all key decision making was colocated. The emerging model – which has in reality been emerging for probably thirty years – suggests a much more geographically dispersed value chain. Xerox has R&D units in the US, Canada, the UK and France. Volvo has manufacturing in Sweden, Belgium, Holland, Canada and five Asian countries. ABB, the quintessential modern MNC, has global business units in about ten countries. All this is well known, and so much part of the contemporary business environment that researchers have shifted from questions of whether to disperse activities, to how dispersed activities can best be organized. Indeed the challenge nowadays is to find examples of MNCs that do *not* have dispersed value-adding activities.

But what factors caused this dispersal of value-adding activities? The conventional wisdom, and the opening paragraph of this chapter, would highlight the various facets of globalization, such as regional trade agreements, technological changes, converging consumer tastes, new international competitors and so on. The emergent species of MNC, it is argued, can be seen as an adaptive response to changes in the global business environment – if customers, competitors and suppliers are now global, the MNC itself should reflect that geographical dispersal. Previously concentrated MNCs, such as Caterpillar and Matsushita, have indeed shifted manufacturing and even some development work abroad.

Working from an internally driven change perspective, however, provides a rather different interpretation of the phenomenon of geographic dispersal. Back in 1981, Yves Doz and C.K. Prahalad observed that foreign subsidiaries, as they develop resources in their local market, gradually reduce their dependence on the parent company and gain *de facto* control over their own destiny. Fuji Xerox, for example, started life as a sales and marketing company, and only began doing development work because it needed copiers that could cope with the very thin paper often used in Japan. But this R&D operation, by virtue of its location in a leading-edge cluster of competitors, soon took on a life of its own and is now acknowledged by Xerox managers as more advanced in colour copying than anything in the US. The result, then, was a major R&D presence in Japan, and yet another piece of evidence that effective MNCs tend to disperse their value-adding activities around the world. But the process was facilitated through the bottom-up efforts of managers in Fuji Xerox and *not* through the top-down directives of parent company managers in the US.

In summary then, the observed changes in MNC strategy and structure are as much internally driven as they are externally imposed. In particular, the managers of foreign subsidiaries are instrumental in a process of organizational transformation that has resulted, in broad terms, in the

Old model   **New model**

```
                                        ┌──────────────────┐
                                        │ Global business  │
                                        │   environment    │
                                        └──────────────────┘
                                                 ↕
 ┌──────────────────┐
 │ Global business  │           ┌ ─ ─ ─ ─ ─ ─ ─ ─ ─ ┐
 │   environment    │           ┆ ┌──────────────┐  ┆
 └──────────────────┘           ┆ │Parent company│  ┆
          │                     ┆ │   managers   │  ┆
          │                     ┆ └──────────────┘  ┆
          ↓                     ┆    │         ↑    ┆
 ┌──────────────────┐           ┆    ↓         │    ┆
 │    Form of       │           ┆ ┌──────────────┐  ┆
 │  multinational   │           ┆ │  Subsidiary  │  ┆
 │  corporation     │           ┆ │   managers   │  ┆
 └──────────────────┘           ┆ └──────────────┘  ┆
                                └ ─ ─ ─ ─ ─ ─ ─ ─ ─ ┘
                                Form of multinational corporation
```

Figure 1.1 *Drivers of change in the multinational corporation*

shift of marketing, manufacturing, R&D and even business management functions away from the traditional centre. Unmistakably, this process can also be explained as a response to environmental change, but the point is that we have to move away from a monolithic model in which the MNC (as a whole) responds to environmental shifts, and towards one in which the structure of the MNC is created by the interplay between the actions of parent company and subsidiary managers, who both respond to and drive changes in the business environment (see Figure 1.1).

This is not a novel insight. Gunnar Hedlund and colleagues (Hedlund, 1986; Hedlund and Rolander, 1990), in particular, have done a very good job of explaining how the 'new model' in Figure 1.1 works, and the well known studies by Chris Bartlett and Sumantra Ghoshal (1986, 1989) also provide clear evidence that subsidiary managers have a substantial role to play in the emergence of new organizational responses in MNCs. Nonetheless this represents the true starting point for the ideas presented in the book. Others have examined how MNCs respond to changes in the external environment; the emphasis here is how they respond to changes from within.

Some background: research on the multinational corporation

The issue of internally driven change in MNCs will be picked up again shortly, but before it is addressed it is important briefly to review some of the recent thinking in this area. There is an enormous volume of literature in existence, much of it operating at too high a level of analysis (the role of the MNC in global trade), too low a level of analysis (various functional activities within the MNC) or from theoretical perspectives that are not conducive to discussions of management behaviour (chiefly transaction cost theory).[1] What follows, then, is a brief and selective review of the MNC strategy, structure and organization literature.

The field of research that is typically referred to as 'multinational management' can be traced back to about 1970. Beginning with the seminal work of Stopford and Wells (1972), the focus of this early research was on broad questions of strategy and structure in MNCs. Stopford and Wells, for example, put forward a framework for understanding how MNCs shift from an international division to a global product or worldwide area structure. Franko (1974), Egelhoff (1982) and Daniels et al. (1984) primarily examined the reasons why certain structural forms are adopted.

Figure 1.2 illustrates how this initial focus on corporate-level strategy and structure has evolved over the years. The studies noted above are positioned in cell 1 – they were undertaken at the head office level of analysis and they were based on a traditional hierarchical model of the MNC.[2] This line of research continued through much of the 1980s, but it was then eclipsed by other approaches that seemed to offer greater potential.

The second body of research (cell 2 in the matrix) was concerned with understanding head office–subsidiary relationships. Sporadic studies of this phenomenon were undertaken in the 1970s (for example, Brandt and Hulbert, 1977; Sim, 1977) but the key reference was to a conference in Stockholm at which European, American and Asian scholars brought together a variety of perspectives on managing foreign subsidiaries (Otterbeck, 1981). This research was concerned with questions of subsidiary autonomy, formalization of activities, and coordination and control

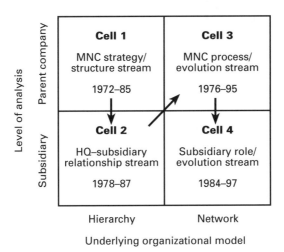

Figure 1.2   *Streams of research in multinational management*

mechanisms. As with the first line of research, it was also based on hierarchical assumptions – that the subsidiary was subordinate to and interacted primarily with its parent company. Research in this vein continued through the 1980s (for example, Cray, 1984; Gates and Egelhoff, 1986; Poynter and Rugman, 1982; Rugman, 1983), but has also lost favour in recent years.

The sea change in thinking that caused both these lines of research to fade away was the realization that the hierarchical model did not capture the reality in MNCs. Foreign subsidiaries often had large manufacturing and R&D activities that were as important as anything in the parent company. And rather than just engaging in communication with their parent company, many had highly developed networks of relationships with other subsidiaries around the world. Ground-breaking research by Bartlett (1979), Bartlett and Ghoshal (1986, 1989), Hedlund (1986, 1994), and Prahalad and Doz (1981) made clear the need for a new paradigm in international management. Terms such as 'heterarchy', 'transnational' and 'multifocal' were invented to describe better the organizational structure of MNCs.

The third line of research (cell 3) can be traced back to the work of Prahalad (1975) and Doz (1976) and followed through the various studies identified above. The focus was clearly on the decision makers in head office, and their ability to structure their worldwide operations in a way that allowed them to get the most value out of their foreign subsidiaries. While never completely disavowing the hierarchical model, this body of research has increasingly sought new ways of describing the MNC. For example Ghoshal and Bartlett (1990) have modelled the MNC as an interorganizational network, and Hedlund has suggested the 'N-form' and 'nearly recomposable system' (1994, 1997). As already indicated, such models appear to be much better descriptors of what actually happens in MNCs, and they have had a considerable influence on my own work.

The final cell (cell 4) is perhaps the one in which most research is currently been undertaken. This line of research is concerned with the foreign subsidiary as the principal unit of analysis, but unlike the earlier work in this area it sees the subsidiary as a node in a network, rather than being in a dyadic relationship with its parent company. Important early studies in this area were the Canadian studies of White and Poynter (1984) and Etemad and Dulude (1986), and the typologies proposed by Bartlett and Ghoshal (1986), Ghoshal and Nohria (1989), Jarillo and Martinez (1990) and Gupta and Govindarajan (1991). In all these studies, attempts were made to identify different types of subsidiary – some with leading-edge strategic roles, others acting as implementers or local sales offices – and then to associate certain environmental or structural patterns with each type.

The more recent variant of cell 4 research is to take a more dynamic perspective and to think about how subsidiaries actually change their roles over time. Research on Canadian subsidiaries, for example, has for a long time sought to understand how 'world product mandates' are gained (for example, Crookell, 1986, 1990; Rugman and Bennett, 1982; Science Council of Canada, 1980). The answer, it seems, is a long process of capability and credibility building in the subsidiary company, coupled with a significant amount of luck. Studies of subsidiary roles have begun to consider changes along the standard dimensions (for example, Jarillo and Martinez, 1990; Taggart, 1996, 1997). And a parallel line of research on the evolution of MNCs (as a whole) has also informed thinking about trajectories of development in subsidiaries (Kogut and Zander, 1992, 1995; Malnight, 1994, 1996).

I have chosen not to mention any of my own research in this brief review, but it should be obvious that it falls unambiguously into cell 4 – undertaken at the subsidiary level of analysis, and based on a network conception of the MNC. Consistent with the latter group of studies, the focus is on process issues, and on the way in which action taken within the subsidiary can influence its role in the corporation. However the focus is also broader than that of most research in this area, in that it is also concerned with understanding how such subsidiary actions can affect the overall strategy and structure of the MNC.

The empirical origins: the 1989 Free Trade Agreement

An alternative way of defining the scope of this book is to describe how I developed my own line of research into MNC subsidiaries. In the early days of my doctoral studies I became interested in foreign-owned subsidiary companies in Canada as they came to grips with the recently announced (1989) Free Trade Agreement with the US. These subsidiaries had grown up, in the post-war years, in a relatively closed economic environment. Tariff barriers between Canada and the rest of the world were high, and foreign MNCs had been encouraged by the Canadian government to create 'miniature replicas' of themselves – subsidiaries that developed, manufactured and marketed products exclusively for the Canadian marketplace. These subsidiaries remained quite closely controlled by their parent companies, and showed little sign of initiative in developing their own strategies (D'Cruz, 1986; Rugman and Douglas, 1986).

The free trade movement, as it picked up steam in the 1980s, presented an enormous threat to these Canadian subsidiaries. What use was a manufacturing plant producing 200 000 units per year when the parent company had another, just across the border, producing two million of the exact same units? What value were the 200 people working in the Toronto head office adding that could not be done just as well by the global headquarters operation in New York? Many observers, even those who supported the FTA in every other respect, forecast that it would trigger a wave of plant closures in Canada's foreign owned sector, and a wholesale migration of jobs across the border into the US.

But the reality has turned out somewhat differently. Certainly there are many cases of US-based MNCs that chose to close their Canadian plants and head offices, but there are also many cases of Canadian subsidiaries that emerged from the consolidation process stronger than they were before. One classic example is Honeywell, a leading global manufacturer of industrial controls and thermostats. Back in 1986, Honeywell Canada's managers realized that their branch-plant manufacturing operation was likely to be closed if the Free Trade Agreement was signed. Rather than accept this eventuality, their approach was to identify and build on the three product lines that they believed were internationally competitive. They presented a proposal to the parent company that would allow them to expand production for these three product lines to the whole of North America, while the remaining ten products lines would be phased out in Canada and sourced out of the US. The proposal eventually went through, the rationalization was implemented, and the Canadian plant emerged stronger than before.

Subsidiary initiative: the core concept

The Honeywell Canada story is about what is referred to in this book as *subsidiary initiative* – the proactive and deliberate pursuit of a new business opportunity by a subsidiary company, undertaken with a view to expanding the subsidiary's scope of responsibility in a manner consistent with the strategic goals of the MNC. Canada in the pre- and post-free trade era was an obvious place to study subsidiary initiative because subsidiary managers were facing an environmental change that threatened the existence of their (subsidiary) companies. But the phenomenon of subsidiary initiative is much more widespread than that. Evidence of it can be found in countries and corporations of all types. And in a more generic form, evidence for it can be found in the academic literature on corporate entrepreneurship.

The empirical foundation of this book, in fact, is really this phenomenon of subsidiary initiative. In the chapters that follow the phenomenon is described in more detail and then its implications are described at increasing levels of abstraction – for the subsidiary company, for the parent–subsidiary relationship, and for the strategy and structure of the MNC. The evidence is detailed and in some ways rather complex, but the basic arguments are straightforward. The purpose of the remainder of Chapter 1 is therefore to summarize the key arguments that are elaborated on in the rest of the book. Figure 1.3 illustrates the flow of the chapters and the themes of each.

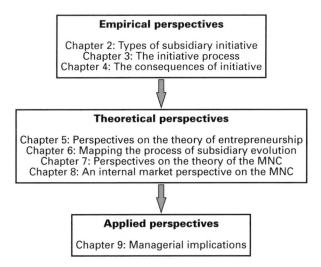

Figure 1.3 *Flow of chapters in the book*

The book in outline

The book splits naturally into three sections, though they are of very different lengths. The first section, on empirical perspectives, provides a detailed description of the subsidiary initiative phenomenon, drawn primarily from my own research. It examines types of subsidiary initiative, the underlying process through which they transpire, and the way in which subsidiary initiatives influence the process of subsidiary development.

The second section, on theoretical perspectives, takes a broad sweep through a number of different theories with a view to explaining how the concept of subsidiary initiative can shed new light on those theories. Thus Chapter 5 considers theories of entrepreneurship, Chapter 6 looks at the process of subsidiary evolution, and Chapters 7 and 8 consider the various theories of the MNC.

The third and shortest section, on applied perspectives, considers the implications of the ideas in the book for management – at both the subsidiary and HQ levels.

Empirical perspectives

Chapter 2 puts forward a typology of initiatives. Building on the network conceptualization of the MNC, the subsidiary sits at the interface of three markets: (1) the local market, customers, suppliers and the like; (2) the internal market, other subsidiaries and divisions within the multinational network; and (3) the global market, which comprises any other customers or suppliers not covered in the first two groups. Each of these markets represents a latent set of opportunities to which the subsidiary can respond. Thus we can identify three generic forms of initiative: local market initiative, global market initiative and internal market initiative, respectively. A fourth type – global–internal hybrid – emerges from the empirical research. Chapter 2 then goes through each of these initiatives in turn, picking out their salient characteristics and describing the impact they have on the MNC as a whole.

In Chapter 3 the initiative process – the sequence of actions taken by subsidiary and HQ managers that result in its success or failure – is described in detail. One important element of this chapter is that it explicitly considers the resistance to the initiative that is encountered along the way, a set of forces referred to here as the *corporate immune system*. This term is deliberately provocative in its suggestion that subsidiary initiatives are treated like alien bodies by the corporate system as a whole. But it is also useful because it provides a framework for understanding the disparate set of forces acting against the subsidiary manager and his or her initiatives.

Chapter 3 looks at the predispositions of the corporate management and the manifestations of the corporate immune system, and then at the specific strategies employed by subsidiary managers to overcome resistance. Two approaches are described. One involves confronting the corporate immune system head-on and building impetus through the traditional chain of command. The other involves circumventing the system and building support for the idea through external relationships. The final part of the chapter addresses the thorny question: how can the parent company management assess in advance whether an initiative will be good for the corporation? The challenge, which has both theoretical and practical dimensions, is to design control systems that weed out ill-thought-out initiatives while still encouraging others.

Chapter 4 examines the impact of initiative on subsidiary development, the process whereby the subsidiary expands its scope of responsibilities within the MNC. Two cases are described in detail – 3M Canada, and the development of its globally oriented manufacturing activities, and IBM Scotland's expansion from PC assembly backwards into development and forwards into logistics and services.

These cases suggest that initiatives can best be understood as part of an ongoing development process in the subsidiary. The underlying drivers of this process are then described in some detail. Specifically, the roles of subsidiary-level learning, capability development, changes to the HQ–subsidiary relationship and corporate-level adjustment are all discussed.

Theoretical perspectives

Chapter 5 provides some perspectives on the theory of entrepreneurship in the light of the subsidiary initiative phenomenon. The argument is a complex one, but it can be roughly summarized as follows. Schumpeterian entrepreneurship is a process of creative destruction whereby the entrepreneur, through the creation of new combinations of resources, pushes the economic system out of equilibrium. Kirznerian entrepreneurship, in contrast, is an ongoing process of adjustment towards equilibrium carried out through the 'alertness to market opportunities' of thousands of independent actors. If we model the MNC as an internal market system, then it is possible to make sense of externally oriented subsidiary initiatives as a form of Schumpeterian entrepreneurship, and internally oriented initiatives as a form of Kirznerian entrepreneurship. Expressed slightly differently, external initiatives represent a way for the MNC to build new products and markets, while internal initiatives are a way to optimize the internal network of activities. As argued in the chapter, this insight has important implications for entrepreneurship *and* for the theory of the MNC.

Chapter 6 considers the concept of subsidiary evolution, or more specifically the process through which the subsidiary's capabilities and charter change over time. While subsidiary initiative is an important driver of subsidiary evolution, this chapter also factors in the investment and divestment decisions of the corporate parent, and the influence of various actors in the local economy. Five generic processes are suggested: (1) subsidiary-driven charter enhancement; (2) parent-driven investment; (3) atrophy through subsidiary neglect; (4) parent-driven divestment; and (5) subsidiary-driven charter strengthening.

The identification of these five processes leads to an important insight about the multinational subsidiary – that its evolution and growth can be modelled in a way that is analogous to Edith Penrose's (1959) seminal treatise on the 'theory of the growth of the firm'. In fact it becomes apparent that the multinational subsidiary represents a more general case than the stand-alone firm because the constraints on growth are not just those indicated by the firm's resource base but also those imposed by controlling shareholders (that is, head office managers).

Chapters 7 and 8 are concerned with the theory of the MNC. The approach taken here is not so much to propose a new theory of the MNC. Rather it is to discuss how the ideas presented in this book can shed new light on the various theories that are currently in existence. Three important theories are identified: (1) the transaction-cost economics approach, which sees MNCs as mechanisms for internalizing transactions in the case of market failure; (2) the network approach, in which the MNC is modelled as a set of semi-independent units (subsidiaries) under a common governance structure, embedded in a network of more or less independent actors; and (3) the resource-based view of the firm. The latter has not been given much explicit consideration in the multinational setting, but given its current ubiquity in the strategic management literature, it is important to consider how it applies to the case of the MNC.

In Chapter 7 the transaction-cost economics approach and the resource-based view of the firm are evaluated with regard to subsidiary initiative, and both are shown to have significant limitations. The transaction cost model of the MNC was developed in the era when most firm-specific advantages were generated in the home country. Subsidiary initiative is *de facto* about the generation of new advantages in foreign markets. Thus with some twisting the phenomenon can be reconciled with the theory, but the result is not particularly insightful. The resource-based view of the firm is likewise built around a simplification of the complex reality of the MNC, namely that resources and capabilities are built at the level of the 'firm'. However the current research shows that resources and capabilities can also be built at the level of the subsidiary unit. This insight has important implications for the ways that capabilities can be built, transferred and combined to generate firm-level competitive advantage. The theory, in other words, needs some modifications in the light of subsidiary initiative, but these modifications prove to be quite valuable.

Finally, Chapter 8 provides a detailed discussion of the internal market model of the MNC. This is an extension of the existing network conceptualization, in that it views the MNC as a set of interconnected but semi-autonomous subsidiary operations that are embedded in a broader set of relationships with other actors. The new development here is that the subsidiary is seen as participating in a number of internal markets – a market for products, a market for charters and a market for practices. These markets shape the resource allocation process inside the MNC. They also illuminate a number of new roles for subsidiary-level and corporate-level managers. It should be noted that this chapter is not a fully fledged new theory of the MNC. Rather it is a collection of ideas that flow from the empirical material and together suggest some important directions for future research.

Applied perspectives

The final chapter (Chapter 9) examines some of the implications of the ideas presented in the book for practising managers. The first set of implications flow from the discussion of subsidiary initiatives *per se*. Thus there is some advice to subsidiary managers regarding the sorts of initiative they should take and the tactics they should employ to give them the best chance of success. And there is some advice to HQ managers regarding the systems they should use to evaluate subsidiary initiatives.

The second set of implications is of a more general nature. The evolving relationship between HQ and subsidiary is discussed, and the reason why so many of these relationships are unsatisfactory is explored. Finally, some consideration is given of the *costs* of subsidiary initiative in order to obtain a more realistic balance between the two sides of the debate. Of course the underlying message in this chapter, and in the whole book, is that subsidiary initiative is *ceteris paribus* a good thing. But it still requires careful handling at the corporate level for its promise to be realized.

Notes

1   Clearly there will be many people who will disagree with this statement. The argument made here is close to that of Ghoshal and Moran (1996), who state that transaction-cost theory, despite its evident success in explaining a variety of phenomena, is not appropriate as a normative theory for guiding managerial activity.

2   Hierarchical here is used in the Chandler (1962)/Williamson (1975) sense, in that it indicates: (1) that the costs of coordination within the firm can be minimized by grouping tasks according to the geographic or product markets on which they are focused; (2) that the retention of strategic decision making at the centre (with routine decisions decentralized) ensures that those decisions are properly handled by a group of experienced general managers. Related to that, the efficient allocation of resources requires that leverageable assets (for example, expertise, scarce resources) are held at the centre; and (3) that the development of an appropriate system to monitor and control divisional managers ensures that the likelihood of opportunistic behaviour on their part is minimized (Chandler, 1962: 309–13; Williamson, 1975: 137).

2

Types of Subsidiary Initiative

This is the first of three empirical chapters. Before jumping into the detailed case studies, it is useful to put the chapter into context.

The theme of the book is *internally driven change in multinational corporations*. Unlike the conventional viewpoint that describes corporate change as a top-down reaction to shifts in the business environment, the argument here is that internal agents – chiefly the managers of foreign subsidiaries – are instrumental in the process. These managers are close to the action and typically far from head office, and are therefore well positioned to sense and respond to new opportunities as they arise. Subsidiary *initiatives* of this sort represent an important source of variety, and ultimately represent the seeds of strategic change in large MNCs.

The approach taken in this chapter is to present some examples of subsidiary initiatives, and then to use these examples to put together a typology based on the sort of market opportunity the initiative addresses. The basic argument here is that four distinct types of initiative can be identified, and that they each have different outcomes for the MNC as a whole.

Gerhard Schmid and the RTAP project

In 1985 Gerhard Schmid, Calgary district sales manager for Hewlett-Packard (Canada) (HP), identified an interesting business opportunity. Many of his key customers, the oil and gas companies that dominate Calgary's economy, had wells in remote and hostile environments. These wells were controlled by remote terminal units (RTUs), but there was no systematic way of monitoring, analysing and correcting the RTUs' performance. Several companies had put together their own one-off systems for doing this, but there was no external vendor offering an off-the-shelf package. Schmid thought that HP could fill that gap.

Schmid put together an outline of the market need and why he felt HP was qualified to meet that need, and sent it to HP Canada's business development group whose response was enthusiastic. The fit with HP Canada's long-term vision was strong, so Schmid was given the go-ahead to look into the opportunity in more detail. As he explained, 'I was given the task of putting together a business plan, doing some market research, hiring a consulting firm to help me, to try to put together a business case for a software unit here in Canada.' Working closely with the HP Canada president, Malcolm Gissing, Schmid spoke with a number of the major oil companies in Calgary and Houston, and established that there was a clear need for a software system to integrate the various elements of the oil production process. Shell Oil, in particular, was very interested, and essentially agreed to buy the entire supervisory control package (including remote terminals and communications software) once it was complete in 18–24 months' time. This business was potentially worth about $40 million.

Schmid presented the business plan to the Canadian executive group and they agreed to go ahead and build the software product. The only problem was that development activities were officially meant to be aligned to business groups, and not national sales organizations, but at that time there was no obvious business group to which the Calgary development team could report. The decision was made, therefore, to fund the development through a 1 per cent 'uplift' on a portion of Canadian product sales, an established approach when there was no readily available business group sponsorship. In 1986 Schmid hired five experienced people, who put together a product specification and decided on what standards would be used. They then 'locked themselves in a back room for a year to come up with the first release'. By the middle of 1988 they had started to release components of the product, now named RTAP (real time application platform), to local beta customers.

But in 1989 Schmid's group hit a major obstacle. As the first generation product was being finalized they discovered that an HP product division in California was working on a very similar product. While Schmid's 'skunkworks' group had been working on a shoestring budget up in Calgary, this Californian group had 60 people, five times the budget and – most importantly – the official 'blessing' of the corporation. There were significant differences between the products, and Schmid's group were about six months closer to completion, but the feeling among the corporate management was that the Californian product had been given the official charter and the Calgary version should be killed.

Schmid and Gissing, the Canadian president, worked hard to persuade corporate management that the Calgary product should be given corporate approval. They were able to make a very strong case on the basis of their advanced stage of development and their guaranteed sale to Shell Oil. Their tenacity prevailed, and eventually HP corporate agreed to support the Calgary operation. The rival product group was disbanded. And the sale to Shell was made shortly thereafter, leading to a slow but steady stream of customers in North America and Europe. By 1991–2 the Calgary operation was making an operating profit and had worldwide sales (with hardware) of around $15 million annually.

But in 1992 the group's existence was once more under threat. Worried that their development organization was spiralling out of control, HP corporate decided to move to a global pricing model (which made it impossible for HP Canada to continue to fund RTAP development) and to insist that all development work be aligned with business units. This meant that the Calgary group had to find a home in an existing business group, or face divestment. Schmid therefore spent much of 1993 talking to the various business groups in the US and thinking through the possibility of a management buy-out. Eventually he found a willing parent, the Lake Stevens Instrument Division (LSID), which saw a good fit between its product portfolio and RTAP. The match was made, and from November 1993 the Calgary operation was officially linked to LSID. In total it had taken almost eight years from the initial idea until the product was officially sanctioned by the corporate system.

What *is* subsidiary initiative?

In many ways the tale of Gerhard Schmid and the RTAP product is nothing special. This sort of thing happens all the time in large corporations such as Hewlett Packard, and the fact that parts of the story are exemplary (acting on new opportunities; winning over sceptical managers) while other parts are less auspicious (a rival group trying to close down Calgary) is just evidence of the complex and conflicting objectives that MNCs have to juggle on a day-to-day basis.

But in certain respects the Gerhard Schmid story is actually rather unusual. The first important point to underline is that *cases of initiatives such as these in foreign subsidiaries are relatively rare.* Academic studies have identified a good number of cases over the years, but what goes unrecognized is the number of subsidiary companies where the search for such stories has come up empty. Take for example an interview conducted by the author in the UK subsidiary of a German MNC, in which the concept of subsidiary initiative could not even be understood by the general manager. 'New products are developed in Germany', he explained, 'if the ideas we get in the UK market are worth pursuing, the German parent company has probably already looked into them'. Subsidiary initiative, in other words, was not part of the *modus operandi* of this firm. Experience suggests that firms such as this are probably in the majority. Even some parent company managers explicitly acknowledge that they have no interest in encouraging subsidiary initiatives.

Why is that? Everyone knows that MNCs have to 'tap their subsidiaries for global reach' (Bartlett and Ghoshal, 1986) – they have to listen and respond to the ideas generated by their subsidiary managers in multiple and differing markets if they are to reap the rewards of multinationality. But despite such a well-known and obvious strategic imperative, the evidence clearly shows that many MNCs disregard it. In some companies it is essentially a matter of policy that subsidiaries should have no degree of freedom to identify or pursue new ideas. In other companies, subsidiary initiative is officially encouraged but in practice fiercely suppressed through a plethora of forces that will be referred to in Chapter 3 as the 'corporate immune system'. These issues will be followed up in subsequent chapters, but either way we have the odd situation that a phenomenon that is clearly valuable *in theory* is hard to find *in practice*.

The second important point to make about the Gerhard Schmid story is that the initiative was inspired by a business opportunity that arose through interaction with local customers. There is nothing odd about that, one might say. But as it turns out, local customers are just one of multiple sources of opportunity for initiatives. Other sources of inspiration include existing operations elsewhere in the MNC, a corporate business plan that head office managers are looking into, and customers located in a different country. In other words the *locus of the business opportunity* turns out to be one of the decisive factors for categorizing subsidiary initiatives, and for making sense of the entire phenomenon.

Rather than leap into a discussion of the conceptual framework at this point, it is probably worthwhile to take a couple of steps back and consider what the academic literature has to say about subsidiary initiative. Once this has been done, the various types of subsidiary initiative can be considered in greater detail.

Some background on initiative and multinational networks

Initiative, as described here, is a manifestation of corporate entrepreneurship. In broad terms, three forms of corporate entrepreneurship can be identified (Stopford and Baden-Fuller, 1994): (1) the creation of new business activities within the existing organization; (2) the transformation or renewal of existing organizations; and (3) the enterprise changing the rules of competition in its industry. The focus here is on the first of these, the creation of new business activities within the existing enterprise.

There is broad recognition, however, that the generation of new business activities or 'new combinations' (Schumpeter, 1934) alone does not constitute entrepreneurship. A research and development group, for example, has a clear mandate to innovate, but the behaviour expected of its employees falls within established norms and guidelines. Entrepreneurship suggests more: a predisposition towards proactive and risk-taking behaviour; use of resources beyond the individual's direct control; or a 'clear departure from existing practices' (Damanpour, 1991: 561; Miller, 1983; Stevenson and Jarillo, 1990). Kanter (1982: 97) proposed the following distinction between 'basic' and entrepreneurial activities:

> Basic accomplishments . . . are part of the assigned job and require routine and readily available means to carry them out. In contrast innovative accomplishments are strikingly entrepreneurial. They are sometimes highly problematic and generally involve acquiring and using power and influence.

On the basis that within-firm corporate entrepreneurship involves a departure from existing practices or 'a *new way* for the corporation to use or expand its resources' (ibid.), it is possible to induce two distinct models from the literature, which are labelled focused and dispersed corporate entrepreneurship respectively.

Focused corporate entrepreneurship (also called corporate venturing) works on the premise that entrepreneurship and management are fundamentally different processes that require different modes of organization to occur effectively. This is typified by the new venture division, whose mandate is to identify and nurture new business opportunities for the corporation (Burgelman, 1983a; Sykes, 1986). The new venture division is typically a semi-autonomous entity with little formal structure, integration across traditional functional areas, availability of 'patient money' and management support for risk-taking and creativity (Galbraith, 1982; Quinn, 1985; Sathe, 1985). There are many examples of MNCs that have pursued this approach to corporate entrepreneurship, including 3M, Kodak and Exxon (Ginsberg and Hay, 1995; Sykes, 1986). Note that the mandate of a new venture division is fundamentally broader and more ambiguous than that of a research and development group, where the set of tasks and responsibilities can be fairly narrowly defined. In Schollhammer's (1982) terms, the new venture division is a case of 'incubative' entrepreneurship while the R&D group is 'administrative' entrepreneurship.

Dispersed corporate entrepreneurship (also called intrapreneurship) rests on the premise that every individual in the company has the capacity for both managerial and entrepreneurial behaviour *more or less simultaneously*. Rather than hiving off separate groups or divisions to be entrepreneurial while the rest are left to pursue the ongoing managerial tasks (Galbraith, 1982), the dispersed approach sees the development of an entrepreneurial culture or posture as the key antecedent to initiative (Covin and Slevin, 1991; Ghoshal and Bartlett, 1994; Stopford and Baden-Fuller, 1994). The design of an 'organic' or 'integrative' organization creates the facilitating conditions, but entrepreneurship is actually driven by the actions of employees who – for whatever reason – choose to pursue risky or uncertain ventures 'for the good of the organization' (Barnard, 1938: 200). The challenge for corporate management is to instill in its employees the personal involvement and commitment that drives entrepreneurship (Ghoshal and Bartlett, 1994).

Dispersed corporate entrepreneurship therefore assumes a latent dual role for every employee, consisting of the management of ongoing activities *and* the identification and pursuit of new opportunities (Kirzner,

1973). The advantage of this approach over the focused approach is that a greater diversity of opportunities will be sensed, because the entrepreneurial capability is dispersed throughout the organization rather than restricted to a new venture division. The major disadvantage of this approach is that managerial responsibilities typically 'drive out' entrepreneurial responsibilities (Hedlund and Ridderstråle, 1997) because they are more clearly defined and have more immediate rewards. Unless it is well managed the dispersed approach can actually inhibit entrepreneurship.

Initiative is defined in this book as the primary manifestation of dispersed corporate entrepreneurship. The initiative process is bounded by the identification of an opportunity at the front end and the commitment of resources to the undertaking at the back end. One should note, however, that the long-term success of the resultant business activity is a secondary issue. The entrepreneurial challenge is to move from an idea to the actual commitment of resources; the managerial challenge is to make the resultant business activity profitable. It is important, moreover, to recognize that the focused and dispersed approaches are complementary rather than alternative. For example an opportunity identified in a subsidiary may be nurtured and developed in the new venture division; equally, an innovation by the new venture division may inspire further innovation by an operating division.

Initiative in the multinational firm

It is interesting to observe that this distinction between focused and dispersed entrepreneurship is paralleled by the distinction that is often made between 'assigned' and 'assumed' roles in foreign subsidiary units in MNCs. While initiative *per se* is not regularly discussed in this literature, many of the associated concepts are.

Assigned roles. This perspective views the subsidiary as having a role in the firm that is assigned by the parent company. Bartlett and Ghoshal (1986), for example, make the observation that national subsidiaries can take one of four generic roles, based on the strategic importance of the local environment and the competence of the subsidiary. The MNC's structure should then reflect this heterogeneity, so that certain subsidiaries receive, for example, much greater strategic autonomy than others. The subsidiary's role is enacted through the definition of an appropriate set of coordination and control mechanisms.

This model clearly parallels the concept of focused corporate entrepreneurship. Certain subsidiaries are made responsible for innovating or pursuing initiatives, while others are given implementational roles. These roles are enacted through the structural context of the MNC. Thus, as shown by Ghoshal and Bartlett (1988), autonomy, local resources, normative integration and inter-unit communication are associated with creation (of innovations) in subsidiaries, but negatively associated with adoption and diffusion.

Assumed roles.   The second perspective talks in terms of the subsidiary's 'strategy'. It envisions a much greater element of strategic choice on the part of subsidiary management than the subsidiary role perspective. Thus the subsidiary's strategy is constrained (rather than defined) by the structural context, and the local managers have considerable latitude within the imposed constraints to shape a strategy as they see fit. Roles, in other words, are assumed by subsidiary managers, rather than assigned by parent company managers.

This second body of research is predominantly Canadian, including contributions by Birkinshaw (1997), Crookell (1986) and White and Poynter (1984, 1990). For example White and Poynter (1984: 69) suggest that subsidiary managers 'Will have to adjust their strategies to success-fully deal with changed circumstances. . . . Through the careful develop-ment of local capabilities the subsidiary manager can contribute to the evolution of the Canadian subsidiary's strategy.' This is of course much closer to the dispersed approach to corporate entrepreneurship. Crea-tivity and innovation should be endemic to the national subsidiary as the driver of its strategy. The subsidiary has ongoing managerial responsibili-ties but at the same time it has the responsibility to respond to entrepre-neurial opportunities as they arise.

A conceptual framework: initiative and market opportunities

As noted above, an initiative is viewed as a discrete, proactive under-taking that advances a new way for the corporation to use or expand its resources. One other constraint on the definition should also be noted, namely that the initiative has to lead to some form of 'international responsibility' for the subsidiary, such as exporting intermediate products to affiliates or managing a product line on a global basis. This is important as a way of excluding initiatives that are undertaken only for the benefit of the subsidiary in the local market. The whole point of this research is that actions taken in the subsidiary have a significant impact on the strategy and structure of the MNC. Thus initiatives whose impact is restricted to the local marketplace are not considered further here.

As indicated in the story about Gerhard Schmid and the Calgary operation, the origin of an initiative lies in the identification of an opportunity to use or expand the corporation's resources. In Kirzner's (1973) words, it is an 'alertness to hitherto unnoticed market opportuni-ties' that stimulates the entrepreneur to act. In similar fashion, Stevenson and Jarillo (1990: 23) see entrepreneurship as 'a process by which individuals – either on their own or inside organizations – pursue opportu-nities without regard to the resources they currently control'.

From the perspective of the subsidiary, the notion of *a market opportunity* is usually understood in terms of its local or national market. The traditional role of the subsidiary was first to adapt the MNC's technology to local tastes, and then to act as a 'global scanner', sending signals about changing demands back to head office (Vernon, 1966, 1979). More recently it has been recognized that subsidiaries often have unique capabilities of their own, as well as vital links with local customers and suppliers. In such situations the subsidiary's ability to pursue local opportunities, and subsequently to exploit them on a global scale, is an important capability (Bartlett and Ghoshal, 1986; Hedlund, 1986).

But to view market opportunity solely in terms of the subsidiary's *local* relationships is somewhat restricting. It is now increasingly recognized that the MNC can usefully be modelled as an interorganizational network (Forsgren and Johanson, 1992; Ghoshal and Bartlett, 1990), in which the subsidiary has multiple linkages to other entities both inside and outside the MNC's formal boundaries. Viewed in this way, the subsidiary sits at the interface of three markets: (1) the local market, consisting of competitors, suppliers, customers and regulatory bodies in the host country; (2) the internal market, which is composed of head office operations and all corporate-controlled affiliates worldwide; and (3) the global market, consisting of competitors, customers and suppliers that fall outside the local and internal markets. This conceptualization is depicted in Figure 2.1.

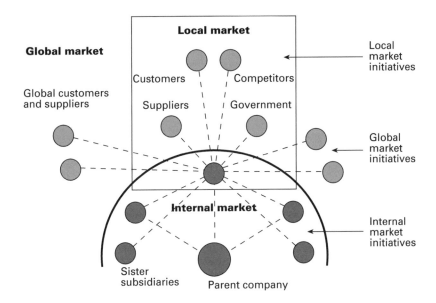

Figure 2.1 *Conceptual model of the national subsidiary and three types of initiative*

The key insight from Figure 2.1 is that the internal market can be a source of opportunities to which the subsidiary can respond. The nature of these opportunities will be discussed shortly, but it is clear that they are rather different from the traditional idea of initiatives being directed towards new product or new market possibilities. It also becomes apparent, when one starts exploring internal market initiative in the field, that two important subtypes can be identified. These are called 'internal market initiatives', as in Figure 2.1, and 'internal–global hybrid initiatives' for reasons that will be explained. The other important insight from Figure 2.1 is that the external market can be divided into a local and a global component, although as will become clear the difference between these two is a matter of degree, not kind.

A categorization of initiatives

Four categories of initiative can therefore be identified. Strictly speaking this is more of a taxonomy than a typology because it emerged through empirical observation rather than logical deduction. However it is possible to be fairly explicit about the dimensions on which these categories differ. The important dimensions are the *locus of opportunity*, meaning the market (from Figure 2.1) in which the initiative opportunity emerged, and the *locus of pursuit*, meaning the market in which the process was realized. In the first three cases the locus of opportunity and the locus of pursuit are coincident, and there is no ambiguity. For the internal–global hybrid initiative, however, the locus of opportunity is global but the locus of pursuit is internal. This apparently odd state of affairs will become clear once some specific examples have been discussed.

The remainder of this chapter will go through the four categories and describe the important characteristics of each – the defining features, the initiative process, the conditions under which they transpire, and the results of the initiative for the MNC as a whole.

Local market initiatives

Gerhard Schmid's RTAP product was a local market initiative. It was identified through discussions with a local customer and then pursued in the local marketplace, though obviously with certain links back to head office for funding and sanctioning. Another example is an organizational change initiated by Philips' UK subsidiary (Ghoshal and Bartlett, 1988). In this case the British subsidiary reorganized its consumer electronics marketing division into three groups: an advanced system group, a mainstay group and a mass-market group. This new structure allowed the subsidiary to differentiate the nature and intensity of marketing support to different customer groups, and it resulted in both lower costs and higher revenues. Subsequently it became clear to Philips at the corporate level that many of the changes in the British marketplace were also occurring in the rest of Europe, and despite some initial resistance the British organization model was transferred to the other countries.

Facilitating conditions. Local market initiatives are facilitated most effectively through a moderate level of autonomy in the subsidiary coupled with a fairly strong relationship with the parent company. In the early stages of the initiative the subsidiary needs sufficient autonomy to be able to apply resources to the opportunity without interference. At the more advanced stage of viability it is important for the subsidiary to have a much stronger relationship with the parent company so that higher levels of resource commitment and sponsorship can be achieved.

The second important facilitator for local market initiatives is a well-established set of capabilities. These are critical to responding effectively to the opportunity as it arises. However, unlike those initiatives that are internally focused, it is less important that these capabilities are in place at the outset. As Gerhard Schmid showed, for example, it is possible to build up the missing capabilities as long as there is sufficient autonomy to act quickly.

The initiative process. As Chapter 3 elaborates in much greater detail, the process is externally focused. Most of the early efforts are directed towards building a viable product or service for the customer in the local market, either using local sources of funding or through partnership with local allies. In the latter stages, assuming the venture has been a success, the challenge is to sell the proven concept back to managers in the parent firm, and building some legitimacy for it in the firm as a whole. This is far from a trivial process of course, but the logic is that an established business case can be more easily sold than an idea.

Outcomes for the multinational firm. Local market initiatives lead in the first instance to new products or services for local customers. However they typically also develop into new business opportunities for the firm as a whole, as the local customer base becomes global. The Gerhard Schmid case is a good example of this. More broadly, local market initiatives can be seen as part of the process of adaptation and renewal in large firms, in that they provide the variety that the firm's systems can then select against. Without the diversity of opportunities and ideas that local market initiatives represent, the MNC's ability to adapt to changing environmental demands would be severely constrained.

Global market initiatives

These are driven by unmet product or market needs among *non-local* suppliers and customers. In theory the subsidiary could interact with any customer or supplier in the world, but realistically such initiatives occur as extensions of existing relationships. Consider the case of Litton Systems Ltd (Science Council of Canada, 1980). Litton developed an international business in the 1960s (through a local market initiative) around an inertial navigation system. On the basis of its worldwide customer base it then identified additional opportunities in related areas, and went on to develop products such as air traffic control systems and radar systems. These product introductions were global initiatives because the locus of opportunity was outside the subsidiary's local market.

Another example is the case of Amazon Canada (not its real name). This subsidiary had a world product mandate, granted by its parent company, for computer terminals for airline reservation systems. On the basis of its existing strengths in this area, Amazon Canada was approached by the Los Angeles International Airport prior to the 1984 Olympics to provide a product that became known as STERM (shared terminal equipment). This product would alleviate the space constraints at the airport by making it possible for different airlines to access the same terminals, rather than having their own dedicated terminals. The point, from our perspective, is that Amazon Canada was no longer just the Canadian arm of Amazon; it was an international business in its own right, free to identify new opportunities wherever in the world they should occur.

Facilitating conditions. The important attributes for successful global market initiatives are like those described for local market initiatives only more so. Thus a high level of autonomy is of great importance, because the subsidiary is typically building on its own existing business areas and needs to be able to act swiftly to develop them rather than wait for permission from head office. As one subsidiary manager trying to pursue such initiatives commented,

> The basic dilemma facing [the general manager of the subsidiary] is lack of investment. If he wants $100,000 to develop a product the customer is paying for he has to make a couple of visits to head office, which might take three months. By the time approval is granted, the opportunity has passed.

The second key facilitator is proven capabilities in the relevant areas. This is perhaps an obvious point, but it bears repeating that the subsidiary will not be trusted to take responsibility for developing global lines of business if it does not have all the necessary capabilities in place. The combination of high-level, proven capabilities and high autonomy typically means, in fact, that the subsidiary operation in question does not have a very close relationship with its counterparts in head office. For example, one individual observed,

[The head office boss] was looking at the numbers, and 'other income' was quite large. He said 'what's that' and [his colleague] said 'that's the electronics group up in Canada'. So my head office boss called me and said, 'we don't know what you're doing up there, but keep it up'. Isn't that representative of the relationship!

The initiative process. Like the local market initiatives discussed above, global market initiatives are externally oriented with little or no contact with the parent company in the earlier stages, and actually very little even in the later stages. For significant investments permission has to be granted, of course, but assuming the business is doing well, that is typically not an issue.

Outcomes for the multinational firm. The immediate effect of global market initiatives is that a specific business area, and the capabilities associated with it, are developed further. Thus each initiative seeks to build a new product or market around an existing business line using the distinctive capabilities of that subsidiary. The term 'centre of excellence' is often used in this regard, the implication being that the parent company and other subsidiaries also stand to benefit from those capabilities. In terms of the broader corporate objectives, this can be seen as another facet of worldwide learning. Tangentially, it does suggest that the concept of worldwide learning is multifaceted, with at least two separate characteristics: (1) the transfer of information about customer needs within the corporate network, as achieved through local market initiatives; and (2) the transfer of proprietary technology and other capabilities within the corporate network, as achieved through global market initiatives. Both appear to be important strategic imperatives for the MNC.

Internal market initiatives

The concept of an internal market initiative is somewhat unusual in that it arises through market opportunities identified in the corporate system. The best way of explaining the concept is through an example mentioned earlier, namely the case of Honeywell Canada's North American product rationalization in 1986.

Honeywell Canada was a traditional branch-plant manufacturer until the mid-1980s. The Toronto plant manufactured control valves, thermostats and related devices primarily for the Canadian market, in volumes approximately one tenth of those of the main manufacturing operation in Minneapolis. In a couple of lines – notably the 'zone valve' and the 'fan and limits device' – Honeywell Canada also engaged in some exporting.

The winds of change in Honeywell began to blow in the mid-1980s, when it became obvious that the Canadian plant could face closure if and when the high tariffs between the US and Canada came down. As one

Canadian manager noted, 'we knew there was no future in being a branch plant operation . . . we knew we had to dramatically improve ourselves to survive'. Proposals were therefore put to the US management regarding the upgrading of the Toronto plant and the rationalization of production, whereby Toronto would manufacture zone valves and fan and limits devices on a North American basis, while the Minnesota plant would manufacture all other lines.

The reaction to these proposals in the US was mixed. Manufacturing managers were understandably negative (they would lose out substantially) but the key individual, the general manager of the homes division, was basically open-minded about the proposal. His attitude was 'let's not be political about this, let's collaborate and do the right thing'. Negotiations followed, leading eventually to the decision to adopt the Canadian proposal. Two lines were therefore closed down in Minneapolis and moved up to Toronto, and Toronto in turn shut down its branch plant operations and focused on its two North-American mandates.

The Honeywell Canada case shows how some market opportunities arise within the existing multinational system. In this case it was the existing internal sourcing relationship between the US and Canada that was inefficient, and which the Canadian management picked up on as an opportunity. By reconfiguring the existing operations, they showed it would be possible for both the Toronto and Minneapolis plants to operate more efficiently. Of course they could have waited for head office managers to come to the same realization, but by taking the initiative the Canadian managers were able to promote a change that was in the interests of both the Canadian operation and the corporation as a whole.

Facilitating conditions.   The most critical facilitator of internal market initiatives is the credibility of the subsidiary in the eyes of the parent company. This is often a function of the subsidiary's existing capabilities, but it can also be achieved through strong personal relationships. As described by one subsidiary manager:

> It is awfully important that we have a close association [with the US management]. We are talking frequently about what are the issues in their business, what are their problems, what are the opportunities that we can offer to help them solve their problems. That is important to do.

The other facilitator, which will be discussed in some detail in Chapter 3, is a global orientation (Perlmutter, 1969) among the senior management of the parent firm. Such managers can be ethnocentric in their approach, which creates enormous obstacles for subsidiary management. A geocentric attitude, in contrast, can end up streamlining the entire process by eliminating artificial roadblocks that are caused through ignorance and disinterest in the ideas coming out of the foreign subsidiary.

The initiative process. Unlike the two externally oriented forms of initiative, internal market initiatives are inherently inward-looking. Thus the primary objective is to obtain formal corporate approval so that the necessary resources are made available. Such initiatives typically involve a high level of selling, first by middle-level managers to their superiors in the subsidiary, and subsequently by the top subsidiary managers to their superiors in head office. This process is encapsulated by the following quote from a middle-level manager regarding an internal market initiative:

> I said really we should make a play for [this business], and started to build the argument. I sounded out the [US business manager]: 'what are the possibilities here? What about running the business from Toronto? What do you think about it?' He basically thought it had merit, and he coached me. But my sales effort was not to try to convince US people beyond my sphere of influence, it was really to get the people here convinced, to provide them a position that they could then embellish. So I worked with them and ultimately [the Canadian President] was the guy to say 'we would like to do this' at a very senior level in head office.

Interestingly this 'vertical' process of building support through the chain of command is often not enough. Sometimes there is a need for 'horizontal' selling as well, so that subsidiary managers can gain the support of peers in the international network. The following quote illustrates the extensive selling process undertaken by one subsidiary CEO:

> First he had to get approval [for the initiative] from the operations committee, who report directly to the chairman. Then he went to the sector meetings, where you had the division VPs. There were three of them. . . . He then went to a couple of other corporate bodies, typical places where you would showcase this kind of thing – the marketing council, the technical council as well, which is a huge group of the laboratory managers. So having cascaded it down he tried to pick large bodies where he would get to the level below division VP.

Outcomes for the multinational firm. Internal market initiatives are fundamentally geared towards reconfiguring and rationalizing the activity system in the MNC. Thus the Honeywell example mentioned above led to the rationalization of activities between Canada and the US, and hence a more efficient corporate system. Equally, such initiatives can lead to certain plants being closed down or moved, or marketing operations being consolidated on a regional basis. In one case, for example, product management was relocated to Canada to be more closely integrated with the associated manufacturing.

The important point to emphasize is that overall sales volumes are not substantially affected in the short run by internal market initiatives. In simple terms, they are about taking the internal resources of the firm and configuring them more efficiently, rather than about increasing the resource base of the firm. As such they can be seen as symptomatic of an overall shift towards geographical concentration by value-adding function in MNCs.

Global–internal hybrid initiatives

The last type of initiative combines elements of the global and the internal types. Like global initiatives, the locus of the market opportunity is outside the subsidiary's home market. But like internal initiatives, the locus of *pursuit* is internal in that it involves convincing head office managers, not external customers. A couple of examples are the best way of making this clear.

Monsanto Agricultural is a leading producer of herbicides. In June 1991 the senior management in Canada identified an interesting opportunity in the corporation's long-range strategic plan, namely the intended introduction in about 1996 of a dry version of their very successful glyphosate technology. Building on the openness of top management in the US to further investment in Canada, these individuals looked into the possibility of bringing forward this planned dry glyphosate investment *and* locating it in Canada. A strong case was put forward, so a team was put together to assess the viability of various sites around the world. Three sites made the final selection list, one in Manitoba, the other two in the US. The Canadian team put together a very creative proposal for a plant organized around self-directed work teams with high levels of outsourcing, and on that basis they were able to convince the decision-making team that they had the best proposal. The plant was built in 1993 and began operations in 1994.

In terms of the process involved, the Monsanto case was rather like the Honeywell case described earlier. Subsidiary managers gradually sought out support for their proposal at head office, and then spent a considerable amount of time showing that they had the capabilities and the cost structure to make the Canadian investment location attractive. However there was one fundamental difference between the two. The Honeywell case was about reconfiguring existing operations; about dividing the pie in a different way as it were. The Monsanto case was about building a new operation, about increasing the size of the pie. Obviously the implications of the two cases for the MNC as a whole are thus rather different. The implications of this distinction will be discussed in Chapter 5, but for the moment it is important to see the internal–global hybrid as similar to the internal initiative but with rather different ramifications.

The global–internal market hybrid can also be understood with reference to an example of a global innovation project. Ridderstråle (1996) examined two global projects each in ABB and Electrolux. One case was Electrolux's decision to develop a washing machine that could be used in both Europe and North America. While the initial decision to start this project was made in Sweden (head office), much of the initial development was undertaken in Italy. US involvement was actively sought in the early days of the project (to ensure buy-in in the US market), but it never transpired. Instead the North American responsibility ended up being assumed by the Canadian subsidiary, which was proactive in getting involved in both development and manufacturing.

Ridderstråle's research shows how global–internal hybrid initiatives play into the broader agendas of corporate management. This project had a top-driven global logic that was perceived to be addressing customer needs, but the way that it eventually transpired was a function of the specific agendas of a number of different subsidiary units. Thus the involvement of the Canadian unit could be seen as a hybrid initiative on its part, but it could also be seen in terms of the overall parameters of the project. Interestingly, subsidiary initiative (in the case of the Canadian unit, for example) can be seen as both a good and a bad thing in such projects. It is good because the active involvement of subsidiaries is necessary for these sorts of project to succeed, but it is bad because the project can be side-tracked towards the specific needs of the subsidiary and away from the global project requirements.

The complex interactions of the local and global agendas will be considered in greater detail later in the book as the ramifications of subsidiary initiative are played out. For the moment it is sufficient to focus on the initiative as an isolated entity.

Facilitating conditions.   These are facilitated by very similar factors to internal market initiatives. That is, the credibility of the subsidiary with head-office decision makers is vital, and this is typically a function of moderate to high levels of proven resources, strong parent–subsidiary communication and relatively low autonomy. One subsidiary president commented on the nature of the bid process in his company:

> You end up with a couple of sites that come pretty close and one that will have a minor advantage economically, but sitting in an operating committee in the States, what really swings you is the credibility of the organization that's asking for the order.

The fact that the market opportunity in the hybrid initiative is typically global has little bearing on the facilitating conditions because the entire process is internal to the MNC. Experience in fact suggests that hybrid initiatives require the highest level of 'selling' of all four types, which in turn necessitates a high level of ongoing parent–subsidiary communication.

The initiative process.   Again, the process for these initiatives is very similar to that seen in internal market initiatives. There is one notable difference however. The distinguishing characteristic is the level of involvement of parent company management, in that hybrid initiatives always have parent management support in principle from the start, whereas internal market initiatives have to build their own support. This creates a rather subtle difference in process: internal market initiatives are iterative, involving several rounds of credibility building with the parent company management and the refining of proposals; hybrid initiatives are 'take it or leave it' proposals in which the parent company management often has to choose between several directly competing courses of action.

Outcomes for the multinational firm.   At one level hybrid initiatives offer a similar outcome to internal market initiatives, in that they are intended to influence corporate decision makers about where internationally focused activities will be located. However, at another level they are very different because they are concerned with large-scale projects, such as Electrolux's new global washing machine. Thus hybrid initiatives can be seen as the subsidiary unit claiming 'a piece of the action' within a broader-scope corporate initiative, whereas pure internal market initiatives are typically smaller-scale projects initiated by the subsidiary unit.

Conclusions

Many of the issues raised in this chapter will be revisited in later parts of the book. In particular the initiative process will be played out in more detail in Chapter 3, and the ramifications of the various types of initiative for the subsidiary and for the multinational as a whole will be discussed throughout the book. At this stage, however, it is worth pointing out a couple of specific implications that can be drawn from this chapter.

The role of the subsidiary in the multinational firm

The first point to make is that this categorization of initiatives provides a new way of looking at the activities of the foreign subsidiary. Taking Ghoshal (1986) as the definitive work in this area, subsidiary initiatives can be focused either on local market opportunities ('local for local innovations') or on global market opportunities ('local for global' or 'global for global' innovations). This chapter suggests – in addition – that initiatives can be internally focused, towards the rationalization of existing activities or the promotion of new ones. Viewed in this way the subsidiary suddenly has the potential to enhance the local responsiveness, global integration and worldwide learning capabilities of the MNC. This is a significantly broader role than previous research has suggested.

How can the subsidiary's entrepreneurial capabilities be most effectively harnessed? The first challenge is to create an appropriate structural context, that is, one that facilitates entrepreneurship. Ghoshal's (1986) research shows that *ceteris paribus* high autonomy, specialized resources, high normative integration and high inter-unit communication are associated with subsidiary initiative. This study suggests a more complex set of relationships. Autonomy, for example, is shown to be positively associated with local and global market initiatives and negatively associated with internal market and hybrid initiatives. Likewise the other facets of structural context actually vary between initiative types as well. The implication is that a single structural context cannot facilitate all four types of initiative. If a subsidiary is highly integrated with its parent, for example, it can easily pursue internal market and hybrid initiatives, but less easily undertake local or global market initiatives.

The implicit trade-offs that the parent company faces in shaping the subsidiary's structural context are reduced when one recognizes that the subsidiary is itself differentiated. One division of the subsidiary can be closely integrated with its parent; another may be largely autonomous. GE Canada, for example, has 11 divisions, each one of which has a unique relationship with its respective parent division in the US. Furthermore the subsidiary's structural context and its assigned role are not cast in stone. Over time a successful initiative-taking subsidiary would expect to change its own strategic context (Burgelman, 1983b) and hence its perceived role within the MNC. One subsidiary, for example, built a new business from scratch in Canada. As the division in question grew it developed an international customer base and a unique set of capabilities, so that eventually it operated as a stand-alone global business. Over this period its emphasis shifted from local market initiatives to global market initiatives, and correspondingly its structural context also changed to accommodate its new role.

In sum, the idea that subsidiary roles can be differentiated through contextual mechanisms (Bartlett and Ghoshal, 1986) is a powerful one, but not without its limitations. This chapter has shown that context needs to be differentiated at the sub-subsidiary level (typically the division, business unit or plant) if the full scope of initiative types is to be facilitated. It also suggests that a more dynamic approach to role and context management is appropriate, given that the subsidiary's opportunity set and internal capabilities are continually evolving.

Key ideas in Chapter 2

- Subsidiary managers are a fertile source of new ideas. Through their interactions with customers and suppliers, they often identify new business opportunities for the MNC to exploit.
- Subsidiary initiatives of this type represent an important source of internally driven change in the MNC. Unlike traditional change programmes, which are driven in a top-down manner, subsidiary initiatives follow a bottom-up process.
- Four types of subsidiary initiative can be identified. One type is focused on new opportunities in the local marketplace. The second type is internally focused and it seeks to make changes within the MNC's existing network of operations. The third type targets global opportunities, that is, those beyond the immediate local market. The fourth type is a hybrid combination of the second and third. Each type has a different impact on the MNC.
- The key issue for HQ managers in MNCs is to understand how to encourage subsidiary initiative *without* giving up control of their subsidiaries. This chapter points to the different systems that are needed to promote the different types of initiative. Future chapters (Chapter 9 in particular) address some of the broader questions about how to achieve this balance.

3

Fighting the Corporate Immune System: How the Initiative Process Works

The purpose of this chapter is to immerse the reader in the *initiative process*, that is, the sequence of events through which new products or ideas 'bubble up' from the lower levels of the MNC. The initiative process will be examined primarily with reference to real-life examples. Where necessary the relevant theory will be explained, but a thorough treatment of the theoretical perspectives on initiative will be held over until Chapter 5.

The darker side of initiative

Nowhere is the difference in perspective between subsidiary and head-office managers so great as in the assessment of new business opportunities in the local market. What the subsidiary manager sees as a great, once-in-a-lifetime opportunity will usually be treated with disinterest or suspicion by the people sitting at head office. In the best-case scenario, the subsidiary manager will find him- or herself – like Gerhard Schmid in the previous chapter – being asked to spend large amounts of time explaining and justifying the business case for the new product idea. In the worst-case scenario the proposal will essentially fall on deaf ears, and no matter what approaches are attempted, the subsidiary manager will find his or her progress blocked.

It should be of no surprise to anyone who has worked in a large MNC that subsidiary managers have trouble getting head office support for their initiatives. But two points should still be highlighted: the extent of the resistance to initiatives on what one could call 'irrational' grounds; and the persistent and somewhat Machiavellian tactics pursued by some subsidiary managers to get round the obstacles thrown in their path by head office managers. One should not paint an extreme picture here because many cases are predictable and even mundane, but on several occasions the author has come across cases in which the subsidiary–head office relationship has bordered on all-out war. Two brief case studies, disguised for obvious reasons, serve to illustrate this point.

The maverick in action

The manager of Datacom Sweden, Ulf Borgström, took control in 1992 of a struggling operation. In the process of orchestrating a turnaround, he realized that the previous strategy of selling only Datacom machines was causing his salespeople to turn away a lot of potentially lucrative business. He decided – without the blessing of head office – to adopt a policy of selling whatever equipment the customers wanted, and very quickly this resulted in a big order of Hewlett Packard machines to a Swedish customer. Of course this news went down very badly at the head office in the US. As Borgström himself explained,

> They were convinced that we were prioritizing the sale of competitors equipment (HP, in this case) over Datacom equipment. We were not of course – it was not a choice of A or B, it was B or nothing! To say the least, this was not understood. Many heated phone calls, hostile videoconferences and top-level pressure were applied to stop us selling HP computers, and go back to selling what the factory could make.

Relations between Borgström and head office became very poor. At one stage the chief operating officer in the US issued a firm instruction that Sweden should fax every invoice and every supplier's invoice for a whole quarter to the US for analysis by corporate accountants, so that they could understand what the Swedes were doing with their margin! Borgström complied, to the extent that he had to, but he also continued with the same basic strategy. As he explained, 'My role here was clear: to explain and defend our chosen route in the face of clear pressure to stop.'

As it turned out, Borgström did an excellent job of turning around Datacom Sweden, and it is currently the single most profitable unit in the whole company. Now, as Borgström delights in explaining, 'Sweden is constantly presenting the case for being an exception to all-encompassing head office directives to catch sinners not saints. And this is usually successful.' Borgström has finally built up a level of trust that enables him to act as he sees fit *with tacit head office approval*, but this is in stark contrast to the dark days of 1992–4, when his actions explicitly went against head office directives.

A frustrating initiative

Pharma UK found itself in an equally confrontational relationship with its Swiss parent company a few years ago. At the heart of the disagreement was an emerging technology that allowed certain drugs to be administered *transdermally* (that is, through the skin) rather than orally. As far as the central research laboratories in Basle were concerned, they were responsible for developing such technologies, and between 1992 and 1994 they worked hard in a joint venture with a major US company to develop their own transdermal mechanism for this group of drugs. But with no success.

Meanwhile a couple of entrepreneurial managers in Pharma UK were pursuing their own development project in this area. Pharma UK had a small group of 60 development people, who had in the past had some success in bringing new drug formulations to market. Jeff Smith, head of marketing for Pharma UK, was aware of the problems that central labs had been having with transdermal technology, but he nevertheless thought he would pursue his own joint venture with a tiny English firm, Morton, using a slightly different approach. Central labs responded negatively to Smith's proposed joint venture on the basis that they were still working on a solution, but he continued anyway. Soon it was apparent to Smith that they had made very good progress. He approached central labs again, confident that they would be impressed by what Pharma UK and Morton had achieved, but again they said no, they were not interested. As Smith explained:

> the central laboratories see Morton as a small, high-risk company. And the in-house experts in Pharma were not impressed, even when I took the Morton people to Basle. I still haven't managed to persuade those people who were sceptical to come over to the UK to see us working. In the early part of the project, what they did was to send one of their juniors over to have a look at the project. He came over with a fixed brief, and tried to change the project guides, the thrust of the project, which would have added at least a year had he had his way. But we keep trying . . . we just reissue invitations to let them come anytime to try to get rid of this political problem.

By 1995 Smith and his colleagues were convinced that they had developed a transdermal technology that was safe and reliable. They tried one more time to convince the central labs that they had a viable approach, but were again rejected. Frustrated and angered by the intransigence of the central labs, Smith then tried a different approach. Through the president of Pharma UK he approached the European market head and argued that the various market companies throughout Europe would benefit enormously from the transdermal technology. The European market head – with a fresh pair of eyes – was able to see the benefits Smith was talking about and agreed to sponsor the UK-based development of the technology, despite the fact that this meant going against the wishes of the central labs. Some years later the transdermal technology became a popular way of administering a number of Pharma's drugs.

Head office intransigence: what is it all about?

While both of the above vignettes had happy endings for the subsidiaries in question, one should not automatically jump to the conclusion that the head office managers in question were being pig-headed, irrational or malicious. In the Datacom case, Ulf Borgström explicitly went against corporate policy by selling HP machines rather than Datacom's own machines, a policy that over the years had served Datacom well. In the Pharma case the decision makers at central labs in Basle had witnessed the problems their researchers had had with developing a transdermal technology, so they – not surprisingly – doubted that a small UK company with a fraction of their resources could succeed where they had failed.

Clearly in both cases the subsidiary managers encountered a 'corporate immune system' that sought to hinder or block their initiatives, but in both cases the head office individuals were acting in good faith, that is, for what they perceived to be the good of the company. Perhaps traces of pig-headedness can be seen – the Datacom manager who did not trust Borgström and asked him to fax over copies of all invoices, the central lab managers in Pharma who did not want to see someone else succeed where they had failed – but even this is a matter of judgement and is coloured by the focus on the perspective of the subsidiary managers.

The idea of the corporate immune system will be defined shortly, but first it is important to consider how one can make sense of the less than flattering stories of head office–subsidiary dogfights. The approach taken here is to start with what may seem a naïve position: that individuals will generally act in the best interests of the corporation. One should not deny that opportunistic behaviour occurs and has to be guarded against, but it is important to consider the argument made by Ghoshal and Moran (1996) that control systems that assume opportunism are prone to induce exactly the behaviour they are trying to prevent. Stated another way, one cannot distinguish *a priori* between initiative and opportunism; rather it is a matter of perspective, and indeed of trust. Thus for a corporation to encourage initiative as a pervasive behaviour, there has to be a fundamental belief that people are acting in the best interests of the larger whole, and not just for themselves.

The other basic point to make here is that head office managers have typically developed strongly embedded world-views that reflect the historical successes of the corporation, *not* the current business reality. One manifestation of this, which will be elaborated on later, is ethnocentrism, or the belief that the best ideas always come from home (they did in the past, so they will in the future). Another manifestation, which the Datacom case hints at, is a basic inertia that prevents corporations from seeing the need to change. For Datacom Sweden, fighting for survival on the periphery of the corporation, it was obvious that it had to be able to sell competitors' machines and shift to open standards. For Datacom head office managers, the traditional business model of proprietary standards and customers for life was still pervasive.

Head office managers, in other words, resist initiatives because they represent a challenge to accepted wisdom. It is a logical and defensible approach, but it is also dangerous if it shuts off the corporation to changes in the business environment. Andy Grove's oft-repeated dictum, 'only the paranoid survive' is shorthand for the same point – that corporations need continually to challenge their existing world-views and respond to changes in the environment if they are to prosper in the long term.

In summary, the initiative *process* is as much a function of the actions taken by head office managers (or their inaction) as it is a function of the proactive steps taken by subsidiary managers. The discussion here has been on the reasons why head office managers resist initiatives, but these are simply the basic predispositions that shape a complex, multistage process of interaction between head office and subsidiary managers.

Having introduced the concept of subsidiary initiative and described a couple of cases, it is now valuable to examine the process in greater detail, in terms of (1) the specific forms that head office resistance takes, and (2) the actions taken by subsidiary managers to fight or circumvent the corporate immune system. The latter part of the chapter will then consider the more practical question of how systems can be designed to make the process work more effectively.

Background to the initiative process

A variety of models of the initiative process have been put forward in studies of corporate entrepreneurship and innovation. A common approach is to divide the process into three phases, whereby the initiative is (1) conceived through the identification of an opportunity, (2) gathers support and impetus as it is pushed through the socio-political organizational system and (3) is implemented. At any stage along the way the initiative can fail to gather the necessary support or resource commitments, and hence fail (Bower, 1970; Burgelman, 1983a; Schön, 1971).

This basic model can be challenged for a number of reasons. The most common criticism is that the initiative process is not sequential. Phases of development are often overlapping; they may be reciprocal; they may occur as parallel or overlain activities; and they may even occur in a non-linear sequence (Burgelman, 1983a; Galbraith, 1982; Imai et al., 1985; Van de Ven and Garud, 1995). It is relatively easy to imagine situations where projects are implemented before they have gained support throughout the organization, or where the process of building support has begun before the initiative has been properly defined. In its extreme form, such non-linearity begins to resemble the garbage can model of organizational decision making (Cohen et al., 1972).

A second issue concerns the criteria for initiative 'success'. One important measure of success is the commitment of resources to a project. Another is the commercial success or market approval of the resultant business activity. However there is also evidence that legitimacy is important, both from corporate management and from other functional areas (Burgelman, 1983a; Day, 1994; Dougherty and Heller, 1994). If an initiative is to lead eventually to a new business activity for the corporation it essentially needs to meet all three criteria. However the order in which they are achieved and their relative importance will vary enormously depending on the nature of the initiative, the structure and systems in the organization, and the industrial environment.

The framework in Figure 3.1 summarizes the foregoing argument. There are three parallel lines of attack that are pursued by the subsidiary unit sponsoring the initiative, directed respectively towards resource commitment, market approval and organizational legitimacy. Resource commitment is the granting of the necessary financial, technological and organizational resources to move the initiative towards implementation. Market approval is defined by evidence of a customer base for the product or service created by the initiative, where the customer can be another unit within the corporation as well as an outside party. Organizational legitimacy means consistency with the established practices and routines of the organization (Dougherty and Heller, 1994: 202). In any given case one or more of these lines of attack may be trivial (for example the subsidiary unit may have the discretion to allocate resources), and at any given time the actions taken by subsidiary management may simultaneously address two or even all three lines of attack. But all three lines of attack are necessary for eventual success. Furthermore, as the following section will elaborate in greater detail, the corporate immune system can potentially act on any or all of the three lines of attack.

The corporate immune system

Almost by definition, subsidiary initiative suggests some degree of resistance from the existing power bases within the corporation. Resistance

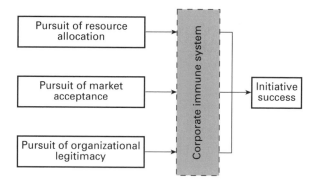

Figure 3.1   *Framework for the initiative process*

can take a multitude of forms, ranging from strict funding criteria to bureaucratic inertia to subtle political manoeuvring. Surprisingly, however, most existing research has given limited explicit attention to the nature of such resistance.[1] The preference among scholars has been to focus on the active process, as manifest in the actions of the initiative champion, rather than the passive process as manifest in the action or inaction of other corporate actors.

But as already argued, resistance to subsidiary initiative is absolutely appropriate. Corporations typically have well-defined procedures for assessing funding proposals so that the most financially rewarding and strategically viable projects will gain funding while others will not. Similarly managers develop informal procedures or heuristics to help them evaluate and choose between the multitude of initiatives to which they are asked to lend their support. In a vastly oversimplified world where bounded rationality constraints and politically motivated actions are absent, one can imagine a process that accurately distinguishes between promising and unpromising initiatives. However in reality it seems likely that errors are made in the selection of initiatives. While these may be both type I and type II errors, the expectation is that they will be predominantly of the type I variety (that is, the rejection of a promising initiative) rather than type II (approving a rogue initiative).

The resistance from other organizational actors can therefore be modelled as a corporate immune system, which is defined as the set of organizational forces that suppress the advancement of creation-oriented activities such as initiatives. The immune system in the body has the task of eliminating or neutralizing any alien bodies that find their way into the system. This system acts to prevent alien substances from affecting the body in a harmful way. However, as in the case of the rejection of a transplanted organ, it is possible that the immune system may reject an alien body that is to its long-term benefit. By analogy, most initiatives, and subsidiary initiatives in particular, face a corporate immune system that views them as alien and potentially harmful bodies.

Why does the corporate immune system fight so hard to keep out subsidiary initiatives? A major reason, as already discussed, is that the mind-sets of individuals in head office are geared towards the maintenance of the existing business model. In organization theory this is typically expressed in terms of creation-oriented activities being driven out by exploitation-oriented activities (Hedlund and Ridderstråle, 1997; March, 1991; March and Simon, 1958). Creation-oriented activities offer less certain and more remote returns on investment, they threaten existing power bases within the corporation and they challenge institutionalized routines and behaviours.

A second reason for resistance to subsidiary initiative is that the ability to gain support for an initiative varies directly with the power base of the championing individual or unit. The classic study by Bower (1970), for example, shows how resource allocation decisions are made on the basis of the reputation and track record of the individual, not the project he or she is proposing. Rothwell (1977) similarly found that champions with greater power and experience are associated with more successful innovations. The consistent theme in these and other studies is that the level of influence of the sponsoring unit is more critical to initiative success than the (proposed) technical or financial implications of the underlying project. Thus the more peripheral the subsidiary, the less the chance of initiative success.

Stated in more neutral terms, the corporate immune system can be seen as fundamentally conservative. Individuals within the system prefer to work within existing routines, throw their support behind low-risk projects and resist ideas that challenge their own power base. Rather than risk allowing a potentially harmful initiative to gain currency, the corporate immune system would prefer to regard all such initiatives as harmful *even if that means a few worthwhile initiatives are rejected*. Of course many initiatives do in fact get past the corporate immune system. Whether that is evidence of a well-functioning system or a testament to the tenacity of the individuals in question is open to debate. But certainly there is no question that head-office resistance will always be present, and that it is – to some extent – appropriate.

The nature of the corporate immune system

Evidence from detailed case-study research suggests that the corporate immune system can be modelled as a two-level phenomenon (Figure 3.2). At the top are the *visible manifestations* of the corporate immune system – the actions taken by individuals at various positions in the corporate system that provide resistance to the initiative. Underlying these are the *interpreted predispositions* of the same individuals, which represent the rationales for the actions that provide resistance to initiatives.

Interpreted predispositions

Three broad groupings of predisposition can be identified.[2] The first is typically referred to as *ethnocentrism* – a preoccupation on the part of corporate managers with their own national identity and their belief in its superiority over others (*Gage Canadian Dictionary*, 1983). Ethnocentrism has frequently been discussed in the multinational management literature as a typical head-office trait of managers from larger countries such as the US or Japan.[3] The trouble is that ethnocentrism is a dirty word in MNCs, so many actions that *are* ethnocentric end up being explained in entirely different ways, even by those individuals who are on the receiving end of the ethnocentrism. For example subsidiary managers

---

Manifestations

Actions taken (or inaction) by corporate managers
that provide resistance to the initiative

•Rejection, delay or request for greater justification by headquarters managers
•Lobbying and rival initiatives by competing divisions
•Lack of recognition of initiative by other divisions

Interpreted predispositions
Underlying behavioural traits of corporate managers

•Ethnocentrism
•Suspicion of unknown
•Resistance to change

Figure 3.2   *Nature of the corporate immune system*

may speak in terms of the ignorance of the head office managers about their country, or a lack of understanding of their capabilities.

The second predisposition is *suspicion of the unknown*. This manifests itself as a reluctance to listen to or to attach credibility to arguments put forward by subsidiary managers with whom the corporate manager is not familiar. As recalled by one subsidiary manager, 'There was initially some scepticism [among corporate management] as to whether the team could do it because we didn't have the credibility in this new business area.' The theoretical roots for this predisposition can be traced back to Simon's (1957, 1976) work on cognitive simplification and bounded rationality. Decision makers, according to this view, develop simplified mental models of reality based on cognitive heuristics and biases (Barnes, 1984; Schwenk, 1988; Tversky and Kahneman, 1974). Relevant biases, in the context of the corporate immune system, are selective perception (that is, head office managers screen out unfamiliar initiatives), conservatism (that is, a preference for tried and tested solutions) and availability (that is, easily recalled events are judged preferentially) (Schwenk, 1988: 44). The implication is that corporate decision makers are essentially biased in their judgements of initiatives, towards individuals or subsidiaries that have been successful before. These biases arise simply out of the need to process complex information in an efficient manner, and in that regard they are distinct from the ethnocentric predispositions as discussed above.

Third, there is simply *resistance to change*. Even when there is openness towards a subsidiary initiative, corporate managers typically have concerns that relate specifically to the effect of the initiative on the managers themselves. Resistance to change has been extensively studied by organization behaviour theorists (Kotter and Schlesinger, 1979; Lawrence, 1954; Watson, 1982), primarily in terms of broad-based changes in structure or organizational culture. In the specific context of the corporate immune system, two aspects of resistance to change can be identified:

- *Parochial self-interest.* Corporate managers resist because the initiative is a threat to their personal livelihood or status within the corporation. In one case studied by the author, for example, the initiative required an entire production line to be moved from the US to Canada. As one manager recalled, 'there was an extreme amount of local resistance, from marketing, engineering: everybody had an ownership of this thing. How could you ship your son, how could you do that? Look at all the things that could go wrong!'
- *Misunderstanding and lack of trust.* This is most commonly experienced when an initiative has to obtain the broad-based support of a large number of corporate managers. In one case, for example, the subsidiary received support from the VP of marketing, but this individual then encountered resistance from other people at HQ because they perceived the subsidiary's initiative to be an intrusion into their jurisdiction, rather than an attempt to make some leading-edge thinking available to them.

Taken together, the three categories of interpreted predisposition represent a formidable barrier for initiative to overcome. In some cases the attitudes of the key decision makers are such that resistance is negligible. In other cases these predispositions can act in a multiplicative fashion, so that for example the possibility of personal loss would exacerbate the level of resistance generated by ethnocentrism or suspicion of the unknown.

Manifestations

The corporate immune system manifests itself in the actions of three sets of corporate actors: (1) individuals in the 'vertical' line of command, that is, with direct accountability for the subsidiary sponsoring the initiative; (2) competing (or potentially competing) divisions; and (3) other corporate units. This is an important point to get across because much of the research in this area has focused on only the first of the three (the vertical line of command). However it is consistent with both the network conceptualization of the MNC (Ghoshal and Bartlett, 1990) and the analogous human immune system[4] to see the corporate immune system as a dispersed function. It is also very relevant for the subsidiary manager's initiative strategy because it highlights the numerous sources of resistance, and the likely form that resistance will take in each case.

Taking each of these categories in turn, the first manifestation is *delay, rejection or a request for greater justification by corporate managers.* Delay typically indicates complete disinterest in the initiative by the corporate management, and possibly a hope on their part that it will not be pursued, while rejection is obviously a more categorical 'no' than delay. For one example, as one subsidiary manager recalled, 'We sent the report to the manufacturing organization in the US and like anything that goes to corporate they kind of say great, and you get some comments back. But the comments were very superficial. This was kind of a "strategic plan for the top shelf".' Request for greater justification is a softer form of resistance, and probably the most common. Typically, corporate managers will see some merits in the proposal, but also have major concerns, such as will this initiative meet our return on investment expectations? Does it fit strategically with our current strategic priorities? And is this subsidiary the best positioned to take responsibility for this particular business case? All such questions require additional work by the subsidiary, and often a formal review process whereby the subsidiary's proposal is considered on a competitive basis against those of other units.

The second manifestation of the corporate immune system is *lobbying and rival initiatives by competing divisions.* This approach is prevalent in corporations that make active use of internal market principles, for example by encouraging sister divisions to compete for the right to make a new product. In these cases the subsidiary typically has the necessary resources to get its initiative funded, but it still has to work hard to gain market approval and organization legitimacy. Such resistance takes two forms. One involves the subsidiary attempting to take a business activity from another division, which not surprisingly results in active resistance. As one subsidiary manager who did this observed, 'they were visibly upset . . . there were obstacles put in our way. . . . I was not welcome back there!' The other form of resistance is when another division is working independently on a product that is in direct competition with that being championed by the subsidiary. This can be seen, for example, in the case of Gerhard Schmid and the RTAP product (Chapter 2).

The final manifestation of the corporate immune system is a *lack of legitimacy in other units.* Legitimacy here means consistency with the prevailing norms of the corporation. Again, lack of legitimacy is manifested in a couple of different ways. First, many initiatives take a very long time to align themselves with the appropriate division or group, and end up as 'orphan' businesses. Second, there is often a lack of buy-in to the concept of the initiative by parent company divisions, even after the initiative is up-and-running. For example it is often argued that the activity in question would have more impact if it were by head office.

To summarize, the corporate immune system is complex and multi-faceted, and represents a formidable barrier to most subsidiary managers. Of course the reality is that there are often pathways through it –

'corridors of indifference' – that resourceful subsidiary managers will be able to seek out and exploit. Let us now turn to the types of strategy that have proven to be successful.

Initiative strategies

As in the previous chapter, it is useful to make the basic distinction between internal initiatives and external initiatives. An internal initiative is an opportunity recognized within the boundaries of the corporation, and an external initiative is an opportunity sensed outside the boundaries of the corporation, such as the need to develop a new product for a large customer in the local market. Corporate entrepreneurship research has traditionally focused on external initiatives,[5] but as will be shown, the distinction is important both for the outcome of the initiative and for the strategy pursued by the subsidiary unit.

Internal initiatives

Internal initiatives arise through interactions between subsidiary managers and other individuals in the internal corporate system. For example they can be planned corporate investments, typically large-scale projects with lead times of many years, or they can be existing activities that are being undertaken inefficiently by the incumbent unit. In both cases the initiative is contested, either by the incumbent rival or by a number of other units seeking to win the planned investment on behalf of the corporation.

Consider the example of Monsanto Canada's Triax initiative. Triax is a speciality plastic that was being made for Monsanto by a US-based toll manufacturer. In 1989 the Canadian subsidiary was looking around for opportunities to apply its flexible, small-lot production capability to new products, and it hit upon Triax as a good candidate. It undertook some trials, which showed that it could produce Triax in a cost-effective way. But it realized that a simple economic argument would not be sufficient. In the words of one manager, 'We had to do some lobbying about our capabilities, our technical competence, to prove our costs were good, which the people in the US were not necessarily aware of. And then we had to fight quite hard to justify the project.' Several formal proposals were made but they encountered considerable resistance, manifested by arguments about why the change would not work, and by passive inaction.

Eventually the management in charge of the initiative asked the Canadian president to use his contacts to gain access to the manufacturing director in the US. This individual was thus persuaded to visit the Canadian plant, and this proved to be the turning point in the initiative.

He was visibly impressed by the commitment of the Canadian plant employees and their level of expertise. He subsequently provided the necessary impetus to get his boss's approval, which led to the decision being made to move the operation to Monsanto Canada's plant. As one individual involved in the project recalled,

> To me the personal interface was key. I remember one incident that happened, that reflects the kind of impression that was made at that time. We had an operator in the polymerization department during the visit, who asked some questions to these visitors. He gave his pen to the director, and said 'sign, sign. . . . Because we need this investment. Just take my pen and sign for the project, because we can make it work.' And the director was pretty well impressed by the attitude and commitment shown. And I remember a few weeks after, he said 'I'm glad to approve the project, and by the way I used your pen', he said to that person '. . . I did follow up on your request, and I used your pen to sign the contract!'

The Triax initiative had a successful outcome. By 1991 Triax was being made at Monsanto's plant in Canada, and the output doubled in each of the three following years.

Key elements to a successful internal initiative

In terms of the three lines of attack introduced earlier, internal initiatives tend to focus on the allocation of resources through the vertical chain of command. Market approval is tantamount to resource allocation because the market is defined by those in charge of resource allocation. And organization legitimacy appears to be a relatively minor issue because the endorsement of corporate management, if it is gained, is sufficiently strong to create buy-in elsewhere. Obviously competing units are likely to resist during the initiative, but experience suggests that this does not create problems once the final decision had been made. The process, in other words, is very clear-cut, involving a single line of attack directed at corporate decision makers.

One aspect of the internal initiative process that the Triax case does not bring out is resistance from competing divisions. Often these initiatives can become something of a zero-sum game, in that the losing candidate gets nothing, or can even face the closure of certain operations. As a result of this the preferred strategy is – where possible – to avoid conflict with the competing entities. There are several examples of subsidiary managers showing that as long as the key decision makers can be persuaded that the subsidiary is offering the most attractive proposal, then the resistance from competing divisions will recede.

External initiatives

External initiatives arise through interactions with customers and other entities beyond the boundaries of the corporation. This situation creates two important differences *vis-à-vis* internal initiatives. First, there is no loser: the objective of the initiative is to create new revenues for the corporation rather than redistribute internal activities. This means that the likelihood of fierce internal resistance is much reduced. Second, the initiative is typically able to start in a much less clear-cut manner. Often the subsidiary will start to work with a customer on a 'skunkworks' project, gradually adding resources as the initiative's viability becomes apparent. Unlike internal initiatives, where the start of the work is clear cut, most external initiatives grow in small increments. Most external initiatives also occur in corporations that have a relatively decentralized approach to resource allocation, which obviously is conducive to the incremental nature of the initiative process.

The dominant approach with external initiatives, then, is to circumvent the corporate immune system entirely in the early stages by essentially hiding the initiative. Subsidiary managers often attempt to generate external market acceptance as a means of proving the merits of their ideas, and subsequently present their initiatives to the corporate management as a *fait accompli*. Resistance comes primarily from competing divisions and other units, rather than from the corporate management, who do not feel the same level of threat.

Let us briefly revisit the case of Gerhard Schmid and the Calgary software development centre, because it illustrates most of the key elements of the external initiative process.

- An opportunity was identified in relation to oil industry customers. Schmid and his team began working as a 'skunkworks' in the Canadian subsidiary, with the Canadian president's blessing.
- Awareness that a division in the US was making a competing product. Schmid and the Canadian president had to demonstrate their progress by obtaining the endorsement of a major customer (Shell) to ensure their survival.
- Once the product had been developed, Schmid had to find a major US division to take over sponsorship of his development group. Legitimacy was still a problem, but eventually he prevailed because the product had established a strong customer base.

In sum, external initiatives tend to be championed according to the technical characteristics of the initiative, that is, by generating tangible evidence that the subsidiary has both the capabilities and the customer base effectively to undertake the emerging business activity. This is in direct contrast to internal initiatives, which can be characterized as being championed primarily through personal relationships and active selling to corporate decision makers. In terms of the three lines of attack introduced earlier, external initiatives are characterized by early market acceptance (by external customers) followed by the pursuit of organization legitimacy. Resource allocation is a minor issue, because most subsidiaries operating with this sort of initiative have sufficient discretion to fund their own 'skunkworks'. Table 3.1 summarizes the contrasting processes in the two types of initiative.

Conclusions: making the corporate immune system more effective

A recurring theme throughout this chapter is that subsidiary initiative is both a valuable input into the corporate system *and* something that should encounter resistance from head office gatekeepers. The problem, of course, is getting the balance right: if the resistance is too severe, subsidiary managers will be discouraged and no initiatives will be forthcoming; but if the resistance is too weak, many inappropriate initiatives will be funded and the corporation will suffer from spiralling costs and uncoordinated activities. Worst of all is the scenario in which the corporate immune systems acts unevenly, and lets through some inappropriate initiatives while shutting out some promising ones. Clearly the balance

Table 3.1   *Summary of processes observed for internal and external initiatives*

	Internal	External
Main organizational contingency	● Centralized resource allocation decisions	● Decentralized resource allocation decisions
Key lines of attack	● Resource allocation critical ● Market acceptance and organizational legitimacy secondary	● External market acceptance and organizational legitimacy vital ● Resource allocation secondary
Critical manifestations of corporate immune system	● Rejection, delay, request for greater justification by corporate managers ● Lobbying and competing initiatives by rival divisions	● Lack of legitimacy in other units ● Lobbying and competing initiatives by rival divisions
Strategies pursued by subsidiaries	● Persistent selling of initiative to fight resistance ● Use of (limited) personal relationships with corporate managers to circumvent and/ or fight major areas of resistance ● Avoidance of conflict with competing divisions	● Early generation of external market acceptance ● Avoidance of all parts of corporate immune system in early stages ● Use of proven market acceptance to fight resistance from rival divisions and other units

here is quite delicate, but the worst mistakes can be avoided if a few basic principles are followed.

The first principle is that initiatives should be viewed, in the first instance, as well-intentioned. As noted earlier, it is next to impossible *a priori* to distinguish initiative from opportunism. However if opportunism is the default expectation the result is likely to be control systems that drive out both opportunism and initiative. Much better, then, is for head office managers to start with a fundamental respect for the intentions and abilities of their subsidiary managers, and to encourage them to present their ideas for consideration.

The second principle is that head office review procedures (the corporate immune system, if you like) should reflect the full diversity of the corporation, rather than being the domain of a narrow subset of corporate interests. In the Pharma UK case described earlier in this chapter, the central corporate labs rejected an initiative from the UK subsidiary, but the European marketing board then said yes. Even if it was not created for such an eventuality, it appears that the European marketing board provided a valuable forum in which the interests of the market operations could be heard.

The third principle in the course of identifying initiatives is that the net should be cast wide by head office managers. The criteria for funding proposals can be strict and the expectations high, but it is important that the system does at least make it possible for new ideas to find their way through from the smallest or most peripheral parts of the organization. Unless this principle is actively promoted, the system will gravitate towards certain types of initiative from certain locations that have historically been successful and – by default – neglect the rest.

It is not appropriate to offer too much normative advice at this stage. This will be discussed in more detail towards the end of the book. In addition, some advice cuts both ways. For example it is obviously desirable for head office managers to be more objective in their judgements on subsidiary initiatives, but the fact of the matter is that everything one does is coloured by past experiences, so some level of subjectivity is both inevitable and appropriate. Even a trait such as ethnocentrism, which is uniformly condemned in today's business literature, is not bad *per se* – it is simply a reflection of the historical home-country-based success of the corporation in question.

Much remains to be said about the promotion and suppression of subsidiary initiative, but to a large degree the question becomes one of the dynamics between the subsidiary in question and its corporate head office. In this chapter the focus has deliberately been on the initiative itself as the unit of analysis, with a view to describing and explaining the phenomenon. The next stage is to examine some of the broader implications of subsidiary initiative for the dynamics of HQ–subsidiary relations, and the evolution of the subsidiary as a whole.

Key ideas in Chapter 3

- Subsidiary initiatives typically encounter considerable resistance from HQ and from other parts of the corporation that are concerned with preserving the *status quo*. This set of forces is termed the *corporate immune system*. Just as with the human body's immune system, it is designed to keep out harmful ideas but it also ends up blocking some beneficial ideas as well.
- The corporate immune system is partly psychological and partly structural. The psychological element is the mind-set of HQ managers who are used to seeing good new ideas coming from the centre. The structural element is the formal review and reward systems that have become established over the years. These systems typically make it easy to veto new ideas, particularly when those ideas come from less-well-known managers in the periphery of the corporation.
- For initiative-taking subsidiary managers, two different strategies are recommended for confronting the corporate immune system. One is to go *through* – follow the official line of approval and build support along the way. The other is to go *around* – build support with customers and other outsiders first, and then present the idea to HQ as a *fait accompli*.
- For managers in corporate HQ it is important to understand how the corporate immune system works. Does it let through too many ideas – good and bad? Or, as is more likely, does it prevent a lot of good ideas from gaining exposure? If the latter, steps should be taken to make funding and visibility more accessible to subsidiary managers.

Notes

1   Important exceptions are Kanter's (1985: 101) 'ten rules for stifling innovation' and Burgelman's (1983a) discussion of strategic context definition.

2   Note that in aggregate terms, these predispositions are entirely consistent with the 'not invented here' (NIH) syndrome, which is defined as the tendency of a project group of stable composition to believe it possesses a monopoly of knowledge of its field, which leads it to reject new ideas from outsiders (Katz and Allen, 1982). The NIH syndrome does not, however, appear to have been subject to detailed academic analysis, so our framing of the concept draws instead from a variety of behavioural and sociological works.

3   Ethnocentrism can also be understood with reference to the sociological literature on nationalism (Fayerweather, 1982; Greenfield, 1994; Kanter, 1996: 132), in that individuals learn to overvalue the positive characteristics of their own group (in this case, the nation) and denigrate those of outsiders as a means of enhancing their own self-esteem. However one should be careful to avoid using the nationalism label because it could apply equally to American and Canadian managers. Ethnocentrism is more generic, in that it represents the attitude of those at the centre towards those at the periphery.

4   Unlike other bodily systems the immune system has no central organ (for example the respiratory system has the lungs). Instead the various parts of the system are spread throughout the body.

5   Though not exclusively. Burgelman (1983c) and Ginsberg and Hay (1995) also make the internal–external distinction, but in subtly different ways. Also, Pinchott (1985) to some extent focuses on internal initiatives, though not in a multinational context.

4

The Consequences of Initiative

After reading the previous two chapters, the sceptical reader might be tempted to wonder what the fuss is all about. Gerhard Schmid spent eight years building up a business that could best be described as a 'tiny' part of HP's global portfolio. Ulf Borgström built a profitable niche for Datacom Sweden as a reseller of other firms' equipment. And Monsanto Canada succeeded in taking the production of a short-run, speciality chemical business off the hands of a toll manufacturer. These stories are hardly the stuff of legend. And for the busy executive at the top of an MNC they are likely to be perceived more as a distraction than as a central plank in the firm's strategic plan.

But the fact is that these initiatives, however small, are vitally important. They are the seeds of change; the first steps on a long journey; the tiny acorns from which great oak trees grow. The immediate impact of an initiative may be very small, but it typically leads to further initiatives in the same or related areas, and over a number of years the process that unfolds can end up having a dramatic impact on the role of the subsidiary unit, and indeed even on the MNC as a whole. The purpose of this chapter, then, is to describe and explain the consequences of initiative in subsidiary companies.

Theoretical background: initiative and context

Before looking at examples of this phenomenon, it is valuable to take a couple of steps back and consider how actions taken in the subsidiary (initiative in this case) are both cause and consequence of the organizational system surrounding them. The first point to make is that the initiative process described in Chapter 3 is a drastic simplification of reality because it is driven exclusively by the actions of subsidiary management. Most processes are not that simple. Head office managers and other corporate actors typically have a major role to play in shaping the process that transpires in the subsidiary. And the constraints imposed by the local business environment can have a significant impact on the outcome. Thus it will become clear in this chapter and in later ones that it is really the *interplay* between these subprocesses that defines the evolution of the specific initiative and the overall development of the subsidiary.

The approach taken in this chapter is to model subsidiary initiative primarily as a function of organizational context, defined as *the set of administrative and social mechanisms that shape the behaviours of actors in the organization, over which top management have some control.* The essence of this definition is that initiative, like any other behaviour, is a function of the setting in which it occurs, and that within an organization many of the crucial facets of that setting are under the direct or indirect control of the top management. Reporting relationships, access to financial resources, reward systems, development programmes and a host of other mechanisms all influence the way an individual behaves. These mechanisms together constitute organizational context (Bower, 1970; Prahalad and Doz, 1981). But the term 'context' can also be viewed more broadly, in that the behaviour of individuals in a subsidiary is shaped by more than just administrative and social mechanisms within the firm. Another important set of cues for a subsidiary firm comes from its *local environmental context*, that is, the set of customers, suppliers, competitors and institutional bodies with which it interacts (Westney, 1994; Ghoshal and Nohria, 1989).

The other point to mention at this stage is that initiative can also affect the organizational and local environmental context through some form of feedback process. As will be discussed later, this feedback loop is typically much weaker than the primary relationship, but the suggestion is that it is sufficiently strong to make a difference – and thus to drive the development of the subsidiary.

The organization context literature

A key part of the definition of organizational context is the recognition that both administrative and social mechanisms can be used to shape behaviour. Thus two very distinct lines of thinking can be discerned in the literature representing these two sets of mechanisms.

Structural context. This is defined by Bower (1970: 71) as a 'set of organisational forces that influence the processes of definition and impetus. [It consists of] the formal organisation, the system of information and control used to measure performance of the business, and the systems used to measure and reward performance of managers'. These forces, in other words, are relatively direct mechanisms for controlling behaviour. Subsequent to Bower's original work a number of studies extended the concept of structural context to include a number of more indirect mechanisms, such as management development programmes and socialization (Prahalad and Doz, 1981).

Behavioural context. This is defined by Bartlett and Ghoshal (1995: 12) as the 'carefully nurtured, deeply embedded corporate work ethic that triggers the individual-level behaviours of entrepreneurship, collaboration and learning'. The central observation here, as well as in many related studies of organization culture and climate, is that some organizations manage to instil in their employees an enthusiasm or level of involvement above and beyond that justified by economic rewards alone. Unlike structural context, which manipulates employees through a system of reward and punishment, behavioural context appears to encourage their involvement at an emotional level. Both shape employee behaviour, but they do so in rather different ways.

Structural vs behavioural context

While structural and behavioural context are substantially different concepts with different intellectual roots, there have been some attempts to combine the two. Kanter (1985) discusses both the structural and cultural facets of 'integrative' organizations; Burns and Stalker's (1961) 'organic' organizations, likewise, have structural and behavioural dimensions; and some of the writing on multinational context management has discussed both structural and behavioural elements (for example Bartlett and Ghoshal, 1989; Prahalad and Doz, 1981). Structural and behavioural context in other words can be seen as complementary, rather than competing, management approaches.

Another similarity between the two schools of thought is that both *see the possibility of initiative having a feedback impact on context*. As discussed above, Ghoshal and Bartlett (1994) see behavioural context evolving in part through the actions of the management and in part through the emergence of entrepreneurship, cooperation and learning as desirable organizational outcomes. The implication here is of a tight reciprocal relationship between context and entrepreneurship. In terms of structural context, a linkage between the two constructs is suggested by Burgelman (1983a), who proposes that autonomous action (that is, initiative) can, in the long term, bring new ventures within the overall concept of corporate strategy, which in turn leads to changes in the structural context of the corporation. The implication, in this case, is that the influence of initiative on structural context is relatively tenuous and occurs over the long term, but is present nevertheless.

The local environmental context

The literature on MNCs frequently emphasizes the point that a subsidiary unit faces competing pressures: for responsiveness to host country demands, and for conformity to corporate norms (Bartlett and Ghoshal, 1989; Prahalad and Doz, 1987; Westney, 1994). In terms of the current discussion this means that subsidiary initiative, alongside other behaviours, is shaped by the local environmental context as well as by elements of the organizational context. Literature in this vein includes Porter's

(1990) argument that the local 'diamond' fosters innovation and superior competitiveness in participating firms; Westney's (1990) study of isomorphic behaviour among R&D subsidiaries in Japan; and Ghoshal's (1986) concept of a differentiated network in which each subsidiary's role is a function of its local environment as well as its own capabilities.

Model development

The starting point for the model developed here is that MNCs have *multiple levels of organization context*. They are typically divided into semi-autonomous operating units with responsibility for a business group, a country or both. Within these subsidiary units there are additional operating units, and at each level it is possible to conceptualize a distinctive context emerging. A large corporation could potentially have three or four 'nested' organization contexts. Employees at the lowest level would presumably expect to be guided primarily by their immediate context (the innermost one), but to some extent would also be influenced by those surrounding it.

Furthermore the nested layers of organization context are not independent. A subsidiary unit may be largely autonomous, and therefore have its own unique context, but it still operates as part of the larger organization. The corporate management have the responsibility to select the president of that unit and define the scope of his or her responsibilities, and this in turn will substantially affect the nature of the unit's organization context. Thus, in the short term subsidiary unit contexts may appear to be independent of the broader organizational context, but in the longer term they are clearly subordinate to it.

Figure 4.1 suggests that subsidiary initiative can be modelled as a function of the subsidiary context, the corporate context and the local environmental context. Following on from the discussion above, the following broad propositions can be set out. Subsidiary initiative is promoted or suppressed according to the nature of the three sets of forces acting on it. Subsidiary initiative, in turn, is expected to affect the subsidiary context and then indirectly affect the corporate context. Note that the relationship between corporate context and subsidiary initiative is, in effect, mediated by the subsidiary management through their definition of a subsidiary context.

What does this model have to do with subsidiary development? Essentially subsidiary development can be seen as the entire process over a period of time, which is punctuated by a number of discrete initiatives. Each initiative (assuming it is successful) represents a significant enhancement of the subsidiary's responsibilities, but in addition it also results in some changes to the subsidiary and corporate contexts. These changes then help to promote or hinder subsequent initiatives. It is

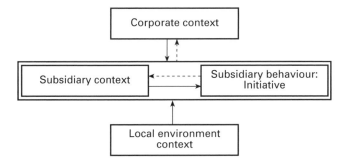

Figure 4.1 *Relationship between organization context and subsidiary initiative*

therefore the entire cycle depicted in Figure 4.1 that constitutes subsidiary development.

Initiative and subsidiary development

Let us now turn to the evidence for subsidiary development and the role of initiative in driving it. Subsidiary development can be understood at this point as the process through which the subsidiary unit builds a set of valuable resources and capabilities. A more exact definition will be put forward in Chapter 6. To introduce the concept, a couple of brief examples will be presented.

3M Canada

3M Canada was founded in 1951 with responsibility for servicing Canadian customers with the full range of 3M products and manufacturing a small number of products on a local basis. In 1972 the Canadian plant in London, Ontario, was given 'swing-production' responsibility for the abrasives business in the US (that is, it would provide extra capacity at times of peak demand), leading four years later to sole responsibility for light grade abrasives in North America. While this was driven by the parent company, it provided a model for the Canadian company to work towards, and it began actively to pursue manufacturing mandates.

Three new plants were established in Canada in the early 1980s, initially focusing on the Canadian marketplace but with an understanding that they had to be viable 'in the light of North America very likely becoming a rationalized manufacturing environment'. In each case the plant manager began actively seeking out opportunities beyond the Canadian marketplace, either through export or by taking over responsibility for products that their sister plants in the US did not want. By 1986 these initiatives had resulted in export sales of around $250 million for the Canadian manufacturing operations.

The growing reputation of the Canadian manufacturing group in the US led, in the period 1987–92, to a series of new investments aimed at upgrading existing plants and shifting more value-adding activities north of the border. Two of these investments were the result of clear initiatives by Canadian managers, the other two were driven more by US managers. These new investments essentially completed the rationalization process in 3M North America.

The third stage of development in 3M Canada involved a couple of investments that were won on a competitive basis against other 3M plants, one in 1992 for a fairly small insecticide manufacturing operation, the other in 1994 for a much larger tape manufacturing facility. Whereas previous investments had been North American in scope, these two were for worldwide production. Overall the growth of 3M Canada's manufacturing operations was quite spectacular, resulting in an average annual growth in exports of more than 20 per cent.

While this description is of course an *ex post facto* explanation of an incremental, haphazard process, there were nonetheless several underlying mechanisms steering the process, including a common vision, the sharing of 'stories' among subsidiary managers, the development of personal relationships with US managers, and the feeling of enthusiasm and commitment that is associated with being on a 'winning team'. Many of the ideas here will be revisited later, in particular the mechanisms for subsidiary development. For the moment it is important just to emphasize that initiatives clearly had an important (though not absolute) impact on the development of 3M Canada. Figure 4.2 provides a graphical illustration of the development process in both 3M Canada and our next example, IBM Scotland.

IBM Scotland

IBM began manufacturing in Greenock, Scotland, in 1954, first making typewriters and then small computers and workstations. In 1981, IBM in the US began to manufacture and sell personal computers (PCs). With the realization that demand in Europe would be substantial, the management of the Greenock factory approached the parent company with a view to attracting the European production of PCs to Greenock. Feasibility studies were conducted, in which Greenock was pitted against a site in Italy, but eventually Greenock prevailed and production started in 1984.

The Greenock plant grew rapidly throughout the 1980s on the back of the success of the IBM PC. However, the management were keen not to stop there, because they were uncomfortably aware that their cost advantages in production might be transient as wage levels in Scotland

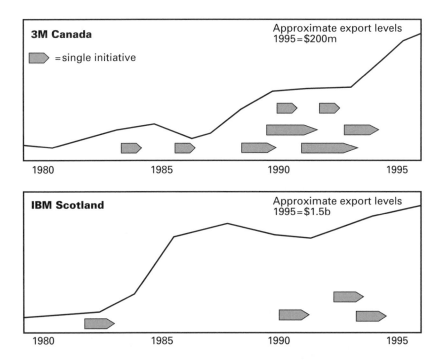

Figure 4.2 *Subsidiary development in 3M Canada and IBM Scotland*

were continuing to rise. They thus embarked on a strategy of 'value chain extension', which resulted in a series of initiatives in the 1990s.

The first occurred in 1990, when they proposed that monitor development, currently being conducted near London, should be transferred to Greenock. Given the parent company's intention to integrate development and manufacturing operations, this turned out to be 'an easy sell' and the shift was made the following year. The second management initiative, a few years later, was a move to consolidate all order-fulfilment work in Greenock. Rather than having one unit in each country consolidating orders and then sending them on to Greenock, the proposal was that this function be handled exclusively at the manufacturing site. Again, this initiative was successful, though it proved to be a much tougher sell because they had to convince all the individual country units that they should give up this activity.

The third and final initiative, also a success, was to create a single European PC help centre in Greenock. Again, this was currently operating on a country-by-country basis, but with the improvements in telecommunication technology it was possible for the Greenock management to make a strong argument that it could be done centrally. Obviously, by locating it in Greenock the call centre could also make use of the existing technological expertise in the factory.

The growth of the Greenock manufacturing site has been quite remarkable. It is now Scotland's largest single exporter and amongst the ten largest exporters in Great Britain, and this development process owes a lot to the attitude of the top management group. As one of them explained, they have always had a certain 'paranoia' that the plant has no god-given right to exist, and that it could be closed at any time. As a result they have always been very proactive in seeking out new opportunities and new ways of adding value.

These two case studies provide somewhat different perspectives on the phenomenon of subsidiary development. IBM Scotland is an enormous operation with export sales in excess of $1 billion, whereas 3M Canada has only around $200 million in exports. IBM Scotland was established as a European manufacturing base for IBM, but subsequently extended its activities forwards into order processing and backwards into development. 3M Canada, in contrast, was established as a Canadian manufacturing operation but over time it transformed itself into a global-scale manufacturer of niche products.

How initiative drives subsidiary development

Of course the theme that binds these two cases together was the decisive part played by subsidiary initiative in driving the development process. In the IBM case, the clear strategy of management was actively to seek out related value-adding activities and have them transferred to Greenock. In the 3M case, initiative was a far more subtle affair, played out time and time again through a delicate process of putting forward an idea, building support for it, trying it out in a low-risk way and then gradually enhancing the parent company's commitment to it. Initiative, in other words, does not just result in a one-off investment, it has a number of longer-lasting and subtle implications for the way that the subsidiary conducts its relationships with the rest of the corporation. Five mechanisms, in particular, are behind this process.

1. Subsidiary-level learning.   A single initiative, regardless of whether it is a success or failure, provides valuable feedback to subsidiary managers. Monsanto Canada is an interesting example of this. During the 1970s the subsidiary began lobbying for a major new investment in Canada, along the lines that 'if it wasn't $50 million we were not really interested'. The best opportunity was a proposed chemical plant in Sarnia, Ontario, which the Canadian management worked on for two years, but this plant was eventually located in Florida. The Monsanto chairman's perspective was 'yes, we want to invest in Canada, but I don't believe this is the right opportunity'. A number of other world-scale investments were also pursued around this time, but none were realized. Then in 1984 a new president was appointed for Monsanto Canada, and he decided to pursue a more incremental approach to investment. His philosophy was 'nothing is too small' as long as the project was strategically aligned with the parent company. A number of initiatives were pursued in this regard, and these eventually led to a series of small investments in Canada in the late 1980s and early 1990s.

At one level, then, subsidiary-level learning is about getting to know the attitudes and the proclivities of decision makers at head office, and adapting the initiative strategy accordingly. Monsanto Canada found out the hard way, but at least it found out. Unfortunately, many other subsidiary companies around the world have made one attempt at initiative, been rejected and never tried again.

But subsidiary-level learning also occurs at a more detailed level, in terms of the various tactics that can be used to bring initiatives forward and garner support. The 3M Canada case provides the best evidence of this. Learning from each initiative was actively disseminated to other plant managers in Canada, such that by the early 1990s they had developed a clever strategy that maximized the chances of success. One of them described the approach as follows:

> The first thing you have to do is get to the point where quality levels are as good or better than the existing ones [in the US] and your service has to be better. This is where we usually make our first inroads, by being more responsive, which you can do when you're a small organization. If you can do that on short notice, then you start getting the sales and marketing people on your side because all of a sudden they have a manufacturing facility that is responsive to them.
>
> And once you have established your ability to produce a product at a cost-effective level, at high quality with good service, then you can start the rationalization process. The argument goes as follows: it doesn't really make any sense for us to continue to make this for the Canadian market because it's really not that much volume, but if we take it out our utilization goes down, so why don't you give us a crack at doing something else that really doesn't fit in very well with your family of products. Then of course eventually you will end up with a rationalized product line being made here for the whole marketplace.

There were many other examples of this sort of learning, where the experiences from one initiative (whether success or failure) were an input into the strategy for the next initiative. An important point, though, is that this sort of learning does not occur unless there is considerable interaction between subsidiary managers. At 3M Canada there was a high degree of interaction, which many felt was one of their key strengths.

2. Subsidiary learning as a sense-making process. Another way of looking at learning is as a 'sense-making' process (Weick, 1979), which in essence is a way of interpreting the past in such a way that it provides a rationale for future action. Sense making is an important and valuable part of strategy making, because it provides an interpretation of what worked in the past, and thus what will work in the future. If 3M's managers deduce that their success is based on starting small and achieving high service levels, then this interpretation will become something of a self-fulfilling prophecy in the future. Furthermore, in the process of articulating this strategy, managers enable and encourage further action in the same vein.

The sense-making perspective can be illustrated further by a comment by the current Monsanto Canada president. He had been very successful in his first couple of years as president, and he explained how he promoted initiative:

> How do you get that initiative? First of all you get someone like myself that says we can do it. You show examples or symbolism that we can change and that we are capable of doing things. You provide the tools, those tools being either information or capability to be able to do it. You provide the support, you get the best possible people in there focused on that. In the case of [the agriculture division] it was really a situation where the talent in the organisation was not in this area. Part of it was trying to bring in an American who had lived and worked in the United States, and we said 'your objective isn't just to run this business; in fact that's part of it, that's expected, now here's the next stage, we want you to get heavily involved with government relations, and answer the question – when you go home at night – how have you added extra value to the corporation for that one share that I gave you?'

This quote clearly underscores a number of steps this individual had taken (building commitment, leading by example, empowering employees), and more importantly the steps he was planning to take in the future. As Weick (1987) has noted, it is more important to have a vision of the future than for it to be the 'correct' one, because vision enables action, and action (particularly when we are talking about initiative) is all-important.

3. Subsidiary-level capability development.   Closely tied to the learning approach is the development of specific subsidiary-level capabilities that are valued by the corporation. These are not the capabilities that are needed to pursue initiatives – they have essentially been dealt with under the subsidiary-level learning section. Instead, what is relevant here are the underlying capabilities that are specific to the subsidiary, and on which the parent company to some degree depends. Thus 3M Canada's capability in small-lot production, 3M Sweden's customer focus capabilities and NCR Scotland's development expertise in ATMs are all vital subsidiary-level capabilities. In Chapter 6 the concept of subsidiary capabilities will be addressed more formally, but at this stage it is sufficient to state a rather simple argument, namely that *capabilities are developed more effectively through initiative than through everyday activity.*

The logic here is twofold. First, an initiative is always undertaken as a means of building something new, as a means of enhancing, adapting or renewing the subsidiary's charter. This suggests that some of the capabilities needed to fulfil the new charter are not already present in the subsidiary. If one takes the case of a manufacturing unit moving from Canadian to North American production, then it suddenly has to enhance its logistics capabilities, its relationships with American customers, its ability to handle multiple packaging standards and so on. By pursuing the initiative, the subsidiary is saying 'we are really good at ABC, wouldn't you like us to take on D as well?' on the assumption that it can fairly rapidly develop the capability to take on D.

The second line of argument is that periods of initiative are great enablers of action, so they facilitate the development of new capabilities in the employees to a much greater degree than normal. Under business-as-usual conditions, capability development is likely to take the form of sharpening and refining existing routines or procedures – valuable processes, of course, but not conducive to the development of new capabilities. During periods of initiative-taking, however, there appears to be an infusion of energy and enthusiasm into the subsidiary's employees, which motivates them to 'go that extra mile'. For example, when it was suggested to one manager that he had been the driving force behind the initiative, he denied it: 'The people in the plant, they made it happen. I was the coordinator. When people believe they are the best they can make a difference. And involving them [was vital]. The only thing I did was communicate.'

There is, of course, a well-established tradition of research into empowerment, goal-setting and 'stretch' performance targets that makes the same point – that individuals will achieve much more if they have a high degree of personal motivation. The implication of the above quote is that initiatives are an excellent way of inspiring personal motivation.

4. Enhancements to the parent–subsidiary relationship.   As Chapters 2 and 3 showed, the relationship between parent company and subsidiary managers is one of the vital determinants of initiative success. Parent company managers are inherently suspicious of the unknown, are resistant to change and to some degree are ethnocentric in their outlook. But if the individual with whom the parent company manager is dealing is someone he or she knows quite well, then most of the suspicion that will normally be attached to an initiative is removed.

As a general rule, subsidiary managers who have actively pursued initiatives have got to know their head office counterparts well, and over a number of years have built up quite strong relationships. However the situation is not quite as clear-cut as that. First, the sort of large multi-national firms discussed here typically have multiple contact points in head office, so personal relationships with one person will not necessarily lend the subsidiary manager any generic credibility that can be applied to others. Second, good personal relationships often provide the initial point of entry, but they are not enough. Many cases involve extensive reviews and multiperson committees. Again, the shift from a few strong contacts to broadly based credibility is a tricky one that not every subsidiary manager is able to master.

Notwithstanding the above, the overwhelming trend in the subsidiaries discussed so far was a warming of relationships with head office managers over the years. Communication increased; the credibility of subsidiary managers with head office managers increased; and there was even a distinct shift away from the ethnocentrism that prevailed before. Perhaps one can say that these subsidiaries finally overcame the resistance of the corporate immune system through their persistent efforts and the legitimization of their capabilities.

5. Corporate-level learning and adjustment. The final mechanism of subsidiary development is the most difficult to achieve. This can be called corporate-level learning and adjustment: it refers to the rather more structural or systemic changes that are made at the corporate level to reflect the enhanced status and capabilities of the subsidiary. In terms of theory (Burgelman, 1983b), the logic is that autonomous initiatives can, over a number of years, lead to changes in the strategic context of the firm, and thus its structural context.

But the evidence that these sorts of change occur is mixed. Of the cases studied by the author, a small minority show clear evidence of corporate-level structural changes as a result of the initiatives the subsidiaries had taken. For example one subsidiary's initiatives resulted in three significant product development groups outside the home country, which in turn led to the establishment of a new corporate funding system for global development centres. For the others, initiative seems to have had little or no tangible impact at the corporate level. One reason for this is simply that the subsidiary has a relatively insignificant role in the firm. As one subsidiary manager observed:

> There is a real dilemma for a small facility. The [head office] operation is trying to decide whether the things we do eminently well are the place they want to be. So its a pat on the back and a kiss-off at the same time. 'You guys are doing a great job, that's the good news; the bad news is its insignificant, and we're not interested anymore. . . . And don't delude yourself that you're important just because you're doing things well.'

To conclude this discussion, a number of different processes have been addressed here, with a view to explaining some of the bigger changes that result from subsidiary initiative. The argument, in a nutshell, is that the series of initiatives that 3M Canada and IBM Scotland took during the period of study were driven by some sort of underlying logic that meant every successive initiative built on those that had gone before. The key conclusion is that the process of development is built very much on the 'softer' elements of the organizational system – the development of close relationships with parent company managers, an internal learning process in the subsidiary – backed up by a more tangible build-up of unique and valuable capabilities in the subsidiary. The lack of evidence for corporate-level learning and adjustment, however, is indicative that subsidiary initiative *per se* is not telling us the whole story. There are a lot of other factors at work, and these are investigated thoroughly in Chapter 6.

Key ideas in Chapter 4

- Subsidiary initiative is an important driver of the process of *subsidiary development* – through which the subsidiary expands its scope of activities and responsibilities within the MNC. There are many examples of subsidiaries that have developed world-class manufacturing operations or entirely new business units (for example 3M Canada and IBM Scotland), and if these are traced back over time there is almost always a strong component of subsidiary initiative in their evolution.
- But it is important to realize that subsidiary development is driven by *three* distinct forces – the initiative of subsidiary managers, the investment decisions of HQ managers, and the opportunities present in the local marketplace. Typically it is the interaction of these forces that propels the subsidiary forward on its development path.
- There are many different ways that initiative can affect the development process in subsidiary companies. The most obvious ways are through the changes that occur in the subsidiary – the generation of new and valuable capabilities, and learning about what works and what does not. There are also indirect ways. Initiative can lead to changes in HQ–subsidiary relations and even structural changes in the corporate immune system, which enhances the possibility of subsequent development.

5

Perspectives on the Theory of Entrepreneurship

This chapter takes the raw ideas presented in Chapters 2 to 4 and examines them in terms of the literature on entrepreneurship. As will become clear, most of the traditional approaches to studying entrepreneurship offer an incomplete explanation of initiative within the large MNC. Thus the objective here is both to identify the areas where theory falls short, and to put forward an alternative perspective that better captures the empirical reality. The chapter is in two main parts. In the first part the various theories are reviewed. In the second part a number of new ideas are discussed.

Theories of entrepreneurship

As a means of putting some structure on the literature on entrepreneurship, let us begin with the simple classification made by Stevenson and Jarillo (1990). They suggested that three categories of research can be identified:

- *What* happens when entrepreneurs act: the net effects of entrepreneurship on the economic system. This is principally the domain of economists.
- *Why* entrepreneurs act: the causes of entrepreneurship. This is principally the domain of psychologists and sociologists.
- *How* entrepreneurs act: the study of entrepreneurial management. This is principally the domain of management theorists.

Of these three categories, the third was discussed in some detail in Chapter 2 with regard to focused and dispersed entrepreneurship. The second is not given explicit consideration in this book because it focuses exclusively on the individual. That leaves the first category – the effects of entrepreneurship on the economic system – although it will become clear that there is considerable overlap between the 'what' and the 'how' of entrepreneurship. It should be noted in passing that Stevenson and Jarillo (ibid.) deliberately avoid making the common distinction between entrepreneurship and corporate entrepreneurship in this categorization. Corporate entrepreneurship is that which occurs within the boundaries of the firm, but in many ways, as discussed below, such a distinction is artificial.

Economic theories: the impact of entrepreneurship on the economic system

The impact of entrepreneurship on the economic system is an important issue in economics, but one which is frequently neglected. The reason for this is simply that entrepreneurship is not readily compatible with the equilibrium framework that has come to dominate the field of economics. As Kirzner (1973: ix) notes:

> The theory of price has once again become the core of economic analysis. For the most part, however, contemporary price theory has continued to be presented with an equilibrium framework. This has not only diverted attention away from the market process and towards equilibrium, but has led to virtual exclusion of the entrepreneurial role from economic theory.

Baumol (1968) makes the same observation but in a blunter way: 'the theoretical firm is entrepreneurless. The Prince of Denmark has been expunged from the discussion of *Hamlet*'. Both these statements, made over two decades ago, are still half-true today. While there is no shortage of research on entrepreneurship, the entrepreneur is still perceived as a marginal rather than a mainstream player in economic theory. Despite that, there is a rich and varied literature that can be traced right back to the eighteenth century (Cantillon, 1755). In an extensive review, Casson (1990) suggests that four main approaches can be discerned in economic theory.

- The entrepreneur as a specialized bearer of risk (Cantillon, 1755; Knight, 1921).
- The entrepreneur as an intermediary in the market process (Kirzner, 1973).
- The entrepreneur as innovator (Schumpeter, 1934).
- The entrepreneur as a specialist in making judgemental decisions (Casson, 1990).

There is not space here to provide a systematic discussion of all four strands of thinking. The relevant approaches for this book are the second and third ones. Schumpeter's (1934) view of the entrepreneur as the agent of 'creative destruction' in the economic system is certainly the most well-known and colourful one, and it is valuable to use this as the 'base case' for the analysis of the role of subsidiary initiative in the multinational firm. But explicit attention should also be given to Kirzner's (1973) thinking on market process and the role of entrepreneurship in that process, because it turns out to have important implications.

Schumpeter's view of entrepreneurship. Schumpeter's landmark book *The Theory of Economic Development* (1934) is concerned primarily with the economic system as a whole. His basic argument is as follows. Much of what happens in an economic system conforms to a 'circular flow' in which the various elements of the system are in static equilibrium. The process of economic *development* occurs when the circular flow is broken. Such changes occur discontinuously rather than smoothly, and they bring about radical changes to the economic environment. The stimulus to economic development comes from within the system through *innovation*, which Schumpeter defines as the carrying out of new combinations of productive resources. This is the process of *creative destruction*. It is the entrepreneur who lies behind this process, because it is he or she who takes the conceptual leap forward to carry out new combinations, and risks destroying the existing order to create something better.

A couple of observations should be made on this brief summary. First, Schumpeter is careful to distinguish between entrepreneurship as a function and the entrepreneur as a person. Entrepreneurship, or 'the carrying out of new combinations', is the process by which economic development occurs. Thus the entrepreneur is any individual who carries out new combinations, whether he or she is an independent business-person, an employee of a firm or a financier. And any individual can be both a traditional manager and an entrepreneur, depending on which function he or she is fulfilling at a particular time.

Second, entrepreneurship is explicitly an equilibrium-destroying event. Schumpeter's circular flow is basically a 'general equilibrium' condition, so entrepreneurship is the means by which the economic system is thrown into temporary disequilibrium, until it gradually settles down into a new, higher-order equilibrium. This contrasts strongly with Kirzner's perspective, discussed below.

Finally, it is important to underline that Schumpeter (1934: 72) envisioned a very broad range of innovations that could be carried out by the entrepreneur – the introduction of a new good or a new method of production, the opening of a new market, the conquest of a new source of supply and the new organization of industry. This list suggests that the process of creative destruction can be initiated almost anywhere. A single innovation will not alone cause revolutionary change to occur, but the sequence of changes that flow from it may. Thus the image that many people have of Schumpeter's 'heroic' entrepreneur – the single individual who brings about revolutionary change to his or her industry.

Kirzner's view of entrepreneurship. The so-called 'Austrian' school of economics is based on the writings of Carl Menger and includes key works by Hayek (1937), Mises (1949) and Kirzner (1973).[1] Austrian economics can be seen as a critique of and alternative to the dominant general equilibrium thinking of neoclassical economics. More specifically, the focus of Austrian economists is on the market process whereas the focus of neoclassical economists is on the system at equilibrium. Indeed a fundamental premise of Austrian economics is that the system is never in equilibrium. The Austrian economics literature is therefore concerned with the process of change in the market, rather than modelling a hypothetical equilibrium that is never achieved.

Kirzner's *Competition and Entrepreneurship* (1973) provides the best analysis of the role of the entrepreneur in the market process. Kirzner argues that market equilibrium is a theoretical abstraction that is reached when all buyers and sellers decisions are dovetailed together. If, however, it is assumed that there is a certain level of ignorance among market participants, a competitive process will be expected to transpire in which buyers and sellers continually revise their positions in search of greater returns. Opportunities for above-normal profits exist, on account of the initial ignorance of market participants, but these are gradually lost as competitors become aware of the opportunities and profits are competed away. Over time the system moves towards equilibrium. Kirzner then postulates that market opportunities are not static, so that the competing away of above-normal profits becomes a never-ending cycle rather than a one-off event. The essence of the market process, according to this scenario, thus becomes the search for previously unnoticed opportunities as the major source of above-normal returns. Kirzner introduces the notion of the entrepreneur as the driver of this process.

Entrepreneurship is therefore defined as 'alertness to hitherto unnoticed opportunities' (ibid.: 39). Kirzner, like Schumpeter, is careful to point out that entrepreneurship is a function, so the entrepreneur is any individual who carries out that function. Indeed he is quite clear that many individuals will play a dual role. They will be managers, operating as price-takers under the prevailing market conditions, and at the same time they will be latent entrepreneurs, alert to opportunities to profit from inefficiencies in the system.

While this is a much simplified and incomplete portrayal of the market process, it captures the essence of Kirzner's argument. Entrepreneurship essentially becomes the driver of the market process, for without it no progress can be made towards the bringing together or dovetailing of supply and demand. And competition is viewed as the flip-side of entrepreneurship, because it is only through explicit comparison of the offerings of competing producers that the entrepreneur becomes aware of opportunities for above-normal profits. Should equilibrium ever be reached, the market process would cease, and so would competition and entrepreneurship.

Comparing Schumpeterian and Kirznerian entrepreneurship. Kirzner's view of entrepreneurship is very different from Schumpeter's in a number of respects, but it also has certain similarities. If one considers the similarities first, it has already been noted that both see entrepreneurship as a function that can be undertaken by any individual. Thus rather than being concentrated at the top of the firm, it is possible for any individual within the firm, or acting as an independent agent, to be an entrepreneur. Second, both Kirzner and Schumpeter focus on entrepreneurship as a process that is central to economic development. Their view on how development is achieved is very different, but for both it is a vitally important activity.

With regard to the differences, the most important is that Kirzner sees entrepreneurship as pushing the economic system towards an ever-receding equilibrium, whereas Schumpeter sees entrepreneurship as the force that pushes the system out of equilibrium. As Kirzner (1973: 72–4) himself notes:

> Schumpeter's entrepreneur acts to disturb an existing equlibrium situation. The entrepreneur is pictured as initiating change and as generating new opportunities. Economic development, which Schumpeter of course makes utterly dependent upon entrepreneurship is 'entirely foreign to what may be observed in . . . the tendency towards equilibrium'. By contrast my own treatment of the entrepreneur emphasizes the equilibrating aspects of his role. I see the situation upon which the entrepreneurial role impinges as one of inherent disequilibrium rather than of equilibrium – as one of churning with opportunities for desirable changes rather than one of placid evenness. Although for me, too, it is only through the entrepreneur that changes can arise, I see these changes as equilibrating changes. . . . Schumpeter's unfortunate emphasis on the entrepreneur as pushing the economy away from equilibrium helps promote the quite erroneous belief that entrepreneurship is somehow unnecessary to understanding the way the market tends towards the equilibrium position.

This is an interesting distinction, and one that is vitally important when one begins to reconcile theory with the phenomenon of subsidiary initiative. Of course, to a large extent both Schumpeter and Kirzner are right because there is room for more than one variety of entrepreneurship in the economic system. We know that industries do go through periods of massive upheaval that can be traced back to Schumpeterian entrepreneurs. But we also know that industries go through more evolutionary periods of adjustment that appear to be driven by the efforts of Kirznerian entrepreneurs. Thus it is not a question of which view of entrepreneurship is correct, but rather of making sense of the two different processes and the effect that each has on the economic system.

The second important distinction between the two views, which to some degree follows from the first, is that the entrepreneur in Schumpeter's world is a heroic character whereas the same figure in Kirzner's world is a rather anonymous individual. For Schumpeter the entrepreneur is the individual who triggers the wave of creative destruction. For Kirzner there are thousands of entrepreneurs, each nibbling away at the small inefficiencies in the economic system. Individually these entrepreneurs have little impact on the process of economic development, but collectively they bring about far-reaching change. But again, it is not necessary to choose between the two models. Both forms of entrepreneur clearly exist, and both have their role to play in economic development.

New perspectives

Level of analysis

The first issue to be addressed is the level of analysis. For economists such as Schumpeter and Kirzner the level of analysis is straightforward: they are dealing with the economic system as a whole, and the role of the firm in that system. Of course the entrepreneur can be anywhere within the firm (that is, she or he does not have to be the owner or the chief executive), but the assumption is that she or he is acting as an instrument of the firm, on its behalf. The firm, in other words, still approximates the 'black box' of traditional microeconomic analysis.

The management literature is far more concerned with what happens inside the firm. One branch of the corporate entrepreneurship literature, for example, attempts to map the *process* of entrepreneurship in terms of the actions and interactions of various actors inside the firm. Chapter 3 of this book is written from that perspective. Another branch looks at the various organizational, environmental and individual factors that are correlated with the incidence of entrepreneurship inside the firm. To some extent this was the approach taken in Chapter 2. These and related approaches are explicitly concerned with the inner workings of the firm, but of course they are less interested in the effects of entrepreneurship on the economic system as a whole. The normative bias is towards making management more effective or business more profitable, whereas the normative bias of economists is towards the efficient allocation of resources in the economy as a whole.

Where does this research fit in? Obviously this is a management book, explicitly concerned with the inner workings of the firm, and (indirectly) with a view to making the management of the multinational firm more effective. But in order to make sense of the subsidiary initiative phenomenon, it turns out that economics is far more valuable than the traditional corporate entrepreneurship literature. The reason for this is that *the MNC can be usefully modelled as an 'internal market system'*. The market dynamics that Schumpeter and Kirzner describe have interesting parallels to the internal dynamics of the MNC. And the subsidiary unit becomes a semi-autonomous entity capable of entrepreneurial action, rather than an instrument of the parent company.

The firm as an interorganizational network

Let us take a step back and examine the validity of the 'internal market' metaphor for understanding the MNC. In some ways this is a very easy argument to make, because there are a number of well-established models that treat the MNC as an 'interorganizational network' or 'heterarchy' rather than as a traditional hierarchical firm. In these models the subsidiary unit is a semi-autonomous entity, loosely controlled by the parent firm and with a considerable degree of freedom to shape its own actions. On the other hand the argument is tricky, because the MNC is clearly *not* a market. The approach taken here – as with any metaphorical treatment – is to use the parallels as a basis for analysis, while remaining conscious of the limitations of the metaphor.

Ghoshal and Bartlett (1990) make a compelling case for modelling the MNC as an 'interorganizational network', by which they mean a network of firms that are not connected by ownership ties. In essence their argument is that 'ownership ties within the multinational do not necessarily preclude the entire range of discretionary behaviours that are possible among interacting organizations that are not so connected' (ibid.: 606). Three points are made in defence of this argument:

- The linkage between ownership and hierarchical power is relatively weak in large MNCs because of large physical and cultural differences.
- The large amount of resources controlled by some subsidiary units gives them considerable power over their parent company.
- Subsidiaries that control critical linkages with key actors in the local environment become more valued by and less dependent on the parent company.

All these points are now well established in the literature. To be clear, the logic is not to deny that ownership of foreign subsidiaries matters, because as Ghoshal and Bartlett (ibid.: 607) point out, 'the parent company enjoys considerable hierarchical authority'. Rather it is to underline that foreign subsidiaries have sufficient freedom in their day-to-day actions for the MNC as a whole to be usefully modelled as an interorganizational network.

The firm as an internal market

But this is really only half of the argument. The interorganizational perspective is very valuable as a means of describing the network of operations around the world that comprise the MNC, but it says very little about the systems used for coordinating these operations.

Hennart (1991, 1993) provides some answers to this question. He starts with the observation, often made, that most transactions lie in the 'swollen middle' between market and hierarchy. In the current line of thinking, this means that transactions that are nominally hierarchical because they are within the boundaries of the MNC also exhibit certain market-like characteristics, such as the use of price control. The reason for this, Hennart suggests, is that hierarchy and prices are alternative *and* complementary methods of organizing. Hierarchy is a good way of controlling individuals' behaviour directly, but it can result in shirking. The price system works by measuring outputs, so it tends to maximize effort, but it can also encourage cheating. Not surprisingly, given their rather different biases, the two are often used in combination to minimize the total shirking and cheating costs. And indeed this is what we see – most MNCs use some form of transfer price system between subsidiary units to monitor outputs, but at the same time individual managers are also subject to direct monitoring, for example through visits by parent company managers or in board meetings.

Taken together, these arguments suggest that the internal market metaphor is worth exploring. Individual subsidiary units can act with a considerable degree of freedom. And market-like mechanisms are often used within the firm to coordinate activities. On the basis of these observations, it is valuable to consider how the economics literature on entrepreneurship can shed light on the inner workings of the firm.

Two forms of initiative

The key insight that comes from bringing together the empirical work on subsidiary initiative and literature on entrepreneurship is that we can broadly *equate external initiatives with Schumpeterian entrepreneurship, and internal initiatives with Kirznerian entrepreneurship.* As previous chapters have shown, external and internal initiatives differ in a number of ways – in the types of opportunity they address, in their facilitating conditions and in the development process. What this discussion shows is that they also differ in terms of the underlying entrepreneurial approach, and thus in terms of their impact on the internal market system that is (in reality) a multinational firm. Let us consider each in turn.

Internal initiative – a form of Kirznerian entrepreneurship. It was observed in Chapter 2 that internal initiatives are focused on opportunities in the internal market system, or the interorganizational network of operations that make up the MNC. These opportunities are things such as a branch-plant factory that needs to be closed down or reconfigured (the Honeywell case), or an R&D unit that is a long way from the associated manufacturing plant (the IBM case).

What becomes clear when one thinks in terms of Kirzner's theory of entrepreneurship is that the result of internal initiative is to push the internal market system towards equilibrium. Equilibrium here refers to *the efficient allocation of resources within the MNC*. Thus, rather than have one plant per market manufacturing a certain product, it may be more efficient to produce it all in a single location. And rather than have a certain product manufactured in high-cost Germany, it may be more efficient to move it to lower-cost Poland and reconfigure the German plant to do something else. MNCs think about these things all the time – not only the cost of producing any given item, but also the relative advantages of one location over another. Whenever one sees plant closures, new investments, changes to sourcing arrangements or whatever, the driving logic behind them is essentially to enhance the efficiency of resource allocation.[2]

This discussion raises an important point – that the resource allocation process in MNCs appears to a large degree to be handled on a top-down basis. The decision to invest in a large new facility, for example, or to rationalize manufacturing capacity in Europe will always be made by the top management, so it is important to ask what, if anything, is the role of subsidiary initiative in such a process?

The answer is that subsidiary initiative has an important role, or to be more exact, two important roles. Let us start by considering the process of rationalization, in which the MNC is trying to achieve the same levels of output but with fewer resources. Obviously if this is a major programme that is driven from above, there is no role for subsidiary initiative. Indeed the parent company team undertaking the programme will typically avoid giving subsidiary managers the chance to become involved, because inevitably each will speak up in defence of his or her own operation. However the rationalization process does not have to be of this sort. Think back to the Honeywell Canada initiative, which led to a reconfiguration of manufacturing activities between Canada and the US. This was a clear case of subsidiary initiative driving a plant rationalization process. Of course it was quite limited in its scope, and neither party suffered too much, but it still fulfilled the same purpose, that is, an improved allocation of resources.

The key point is that if rationalization is viewed as an ongoing process of adjustment rather than something that is carried out episodically and painfully by the top management, then the role of initiative is critical. Plant managers know how efficient their operations are in comparison with others inside and outside the firm, and they have a good sense of what else they can do. If they retain an 'alertness' to opportunities, as described by Kirzner, they can take small initiatives that slowly but surely push the system towards greater efficiency. Whether such incremental changes are sufficient to achieve the level and speed of change that is often necessary in large MNCs is a more debatable question, but at the very least this incremental, initiative-driven process will reduce the need for major top-down rationalization programmes.

The other case to consider is when the top management are planning a new investment, such as a new global-scale manufacturing plant. While the ultimate decision rests with the top management, the process typically provides considerable scope for subsidiary initiative. Think back to the case of Monsanto Canada bidding for the dry glyphosate facility. This was a corporate project, but there is no question that the initiative shown by the Canadian management steered the project in their direction. Another such case was Volkswagen's decision to build the New Beetle in Mexico. This decision was made by the corporate management, but it was arrived at after years of active lobbying by subsidiary managers in Mexico and the US.

This helps us to shed light on the rather awkwardly named internal–global market hybrid discussed in Chapter 2. Such initiatives are internally focused and Kirznerian, in that they are concerned with ensuring that resources are allocated efficiently within the corporate system. But they are global to the extent that the market opportunity is ultimately a new global product for the firm's customers. Put another way, these are actually top-down projects that are being put up for tender. Subsidiary managers can respond to the invitation to bid, or more cleverly, they can become involved at an early stage to ensure that the process is steered in their favour.

So to summarize, internal initiatives are focused on making the allocation of resources within the MNC more efficient. One variety is directed towards getting rid of pockets of inefficient activity within the firm; the other is directed towards the optimum allocation of new resources.

Internal initiative – implications.   Let us now touch on a number of other issues associated with this concept of internal initiative as a Kirznerian phenomenon. First, *equilibrium is a moving target for the MNC*. The processes described are designed to enhance the efficiency of resource allocation, but at no time is the internal market system ever in equilibrium. Free trade between countries makes previously efficient branch plants redundant. And changes in exchange rates and productivity between countries force firms continually to reevaluate the best locations for manufacturing their products. Internal initiative can thus be seen as an important ongoing process that can keep the firm close to its equilibrium position. However the evidence suggests that such initiatives are still fairly rare and fairly limited in scope, so they probably need to be complemented by episodic, top-down rationalization processes.

Second, *the parent company management has to be careful to define the rules of the game very clearly*. It has been argued above that subsidiary initiative helps the MNC to optimize its resource allocation. There is a risk, however, that the initiatives taken by subsidiary managers are geared towards optimizing their own goals, rather than those of the MNC as a whole. For example the subsidiary might put in a bid for a new investment that understates the local labour costs, as a means of unfairly tipping the balance in its favour. This sort of 'empire building' is obviously detrimental to the objective of efficient resource allocation, and experience suggests that it is relatively common. This suggests that the top management in the parent company have to provide very clear rules of the game to ensure that the resource allocation process does not favour cheating.

A third issue that will just be touched upon here is that the *concept of efficient internal allocation of resources is close to Leibenstein's (1966) concept of X-efficiency*. Leibenstein argues that firms operate with considerable slack, with the result that the productivity of many activities lies a long way behind the best practice frontier. Furthermore he suggests that the gains from reducing X-inefficiency are potentially much greater than the gains to be had from improving allocative efficiency in the economy. In many ways X-efficiency is the same concept as my notion of internal resource allocation efficiency, because both are concerned with getting rid of inefficiencies *inside the firm*. But there is also an important difference, in that X-efficiency appears to be about raising the productivity level of similar activities to the best-practice level, whereas internal resource allocation efficiency involves reconfiguring activities between locations. Both reduce internal inefficiency, but they do so in rather different ways.[3]

External initiative – a form of Schumpeterian entrepreneurship. The second half of the story involves explaining the parallel between external initiatives – those directed towards opportunities in the local and global marketplace – and Schumpeterian entrepreneurship. This is much easier. Most people have a better understanding of Schumpeter than they do of Kirzner, and most people will automatically equate subsidiary initiative with the notion of 'scanning' or 'selective tapping' of the foreign market. So the basic argument is straightforward – the subsidiary unit develops an alertness to new opportunities in the local marketplace and on the basis of those opportunities it develops new products or services that end up being exploited by the multinational firm as a whole. Gerhard Schmid's work on the RTAP product (Chapter 2) is one example of this process.

While this is a fair summary of the process, it is possible to do a far more sophisticated job of playing out the concept of Schumpeterian entrepreneurship in the internal market system. The first point to underline is that Schumpeter was concerned with the economic system as a whole and the role of the firm in stimulating economic development. In contrast the approach taken here is to examine the role of the subsidiary in stimulating change in the internal market system (that is, the firm). The analogue to Schumpeter's process of creative destruction, then, is *a wholesale change in the technological foundations or business logic of the MNC that began with the entrepreneurial endeavours of a manager in a subsidiary unit.*

Most external initiatives do not fit this definition. While they fit the simple definition of 'new combinations' that is attributed to Schumpeter, they fall some way short of the rather more strict definition of innovation and the process of creative destruction with which Schumpeter's work is really concerned. Gerhard Schmid's RTAP product, for example, was a niche product that complemented HP's existing product offerings. It fitted easily within the dominant business logic, and it caused no 'creative destruction' of the firm's existing products.

So it is important to acknowledge that many of the external initiatives described in this book are not strictly Schumpeterian innovations. Some set off a chain of events that leads eventually to the process of creative destruction in the MNC, and others achieve the same result but at the level of an individual business unit. But for many others the lasting impact is on the resources and capabilities of the subsidiary unit, and not on the overall business logic of the MNC.

Cases of Schumpeterian entrepreneurship. Let us consider three cases in which subsidiary initiative has sparked off a process that led to major changes in the technological foundations or business logic of the MNC.

First, the NCR plant in Dundee, Scotland, was on the verge of closure in 1980 because of quality problems. Jim Adamson, the new general manager, had a mandate to turn the operation around or close it. At the operational level, he worked on improving manufacturing quality and restoring the confidence of major customers. At a more strategic level, he began to develop a vision for Dundee as NCR's strategic centre for the automatic teller machine (ATM) business. Product development responsibility officially lay with the NCR HQ in Dayton, Ohio, but Adamson began to direct resources towards upgrading and renewing the Dundee product line to meet the demands of key customers. Faced with active resistance from the development group in Dayton, Adamson pursued a delicate strategy of cooperating with them while continuing privately to sponsor Dundee's independent research programme. A successful product upgrade in 1982 was followed 18 months later by a next-generation ATM that set new standards. Dundee's global market share reached 20 per cent in 1984. The following year, responsibility for the global ATM business was officially transferred from Dayton to Dundee. Adamson had secured his vision of a self-sufficient ATM business; and by 1986 Dundee had secured 35 per cent of world-wide shipments, a clear lead over competitors IBM and Diebold.

Second, Ericsson's mobile phone business had its origin in the work of a 12-person development group located just outside Stockholm. Åke Lundqvist, head of this development group, saw the potential for a big consumer business in mobile phones, but his requests for major investment were turned down by Ericsson's top management because they saw Ericsson as a player in the hardware and systems side of telecommunications, not the consumer electronics side. Rather than admit defeat, Lundqvist moved the development group to Lund in southern Sweden so that it would be free from interference by head office. Working on a very limited budget, his team was able to put together a prototype phone that caught the interest of the radio systems business, which eventually resulted in the necessary support to launch the business on a large scale. Fifteen years on, Ericsson's mobile phone business accounted for a quarter of total sales, around $5 billion.

Third, Hewlett Packard's (Canada) X terminal business had its origins in Panacom, a Canadian company specializing in data-management services in the oil and gas sector. HP acquired Panacom in 1983 but a refocusing of the company away from the industrial sector meant that Panacom was without a charter. Rather than close it (which would have been politically awkward), the Panacom management looked for an area with high growth prospects and settled on 'X', which is a graphics protocol used in local area networks. In 1988 they sounded out divisional bosses in the US about the possibility of Panacom developing an X product. Despite some opposition from within, the HP management gave Panacom four months to put together a working prototype, which they did using bootlegged software and peripheral devices from other HP divisions. The divisional executives were impressed, and gave Panacom the mandate they had been seeking. Sales grew from $9 million in 1990 to $110 million in 1993. Panacom was declared the computer systems organization 'division of the year' in 1992 for beating all of its performance estimates.

These brief examples help us to make sense of Schumpeterian entrepreneurship inside the MNC. They share a number of common features. First, *the new business idea challenges the existing fabric of the MNC*. This was clearly so in the NCR and Ericsson cases, though less so in the HP case. Initiatives represent a new way of doing things, and they typically run up against fierce resistance from the business areas that are threatened by them. This resistance was referred to as the 'corporate immune system' in Chapter 3, but in the context of the current discussion it can be seen as an attempt to avoid the process of creative destruction inside the MNC. Either way, it is easy to see why resistance is encountered.

The second common feature is that the *initiative for change can occur anywhere inside the MNC, but it is more likely to emanate from a subsidiary unit*. The NCR and HP cases were driven by subsidiary managers. And in the Ericsson case the initiative started out near headquarters but was deliberately moved away to avoid interference from HQ managers. Subsidiary autonomy, in other words, is of great importance in the early stages of the initiative to ensure that the idea is not killed off prematurely. Later on, however, autonomy can be a disadvantage because the new business idea needs to build legitimacy among the key decision makers in the MNC.

A third common feature is that *all three cases occurred in the rapidly changing computer/electronics/telecommunications sector*. This is not a coincidence – most cases of initiative in more traditional industries are either internally focused or incremental in nature. It suggests that there is an 'industry effect' in operation that is somehow linked to the speed of change in the sector in question. The interpretation put forward here, which will be elaborated on shortly, is that traditional industries move at a relatively slow pace and involve large capital investments that need to be fine-tuned and optimized over time. The computer/telecommunications sector, in contrast, changes so rapidly that success depends on identifying new opportunities as they arise, investing in them quickly, and then staying on the look-out for the next new opportunity. Traditional industries need Kirznerian entrepreneurship to optimize the configuration of their assets. High-speed industries need Schumpeterian entrepreneurship to exploit new opportunities as they arise.

To summarize, external initiatives follow a Schumpeterian logic, in that they represent a challenge to the technological foundations or business logic of the MNC. However, many such initiatives end up being too small to have that sort of impact. Some of this group can be seen as 'failed' Schumpeterian initiatives, while others simply represent incremental initiatives that stay within the existing parameters of the business. It is interesting to note also that the process of creative destruction *inside* the MNC can play itself out in the industry as a whole – for example Ericsson's mobile phone business was a major driver of change in the mobile phone industry. In other cases, though, the internal process of creative destruction has no impact on the industry as a whole. NCR Dundee's ATM business, for example, was very successful but the ATM industry *per se* had already been created.

Extending the model: entrepreneurship and the economics of the industry

The final part of this chapter puts these ideas on entrepreneurship into perspective. It is in part a summary of the ideas presented in Chapters 2 to 5, but it also includes some additional ideas, particularly in terms of the economics of the industrial sector in which the MNC is competing.

The economics of 'increasing returns'

Traditional economic theory works on the assumption that above a certain level of production there will be *diminishing* returns to scale – perhaps because of a difficulty in getting hold of key inputs or because of the costs of coordination. The diminishing returns logic means that successful firms eventually run into limitations so that a predictable equilibrium of prices and market shares is reached. While developed in the Victorian era, diminishing returns economics is still valid in the traditional manufacturing and processing sectors of the economy.

The emerging model of increasing returns is built on the logic that no such diminishing returns to scale exist in the case of knowledge-intensive products and services. As summarized by Arthur (1996: 100):

> Increasing returns are the tendency for that which is ahead to get further ahead, for that which loses advantage to lose further advantage. They are mechanisms of positive feedback that operate – within markets, businesses and industries – to reinforce that which gains success or aggravate that which suffers loss. Increasing returns generate not equilibrium but instability; if a product or a company or a technology gets ahead by chance or clever strategy, increasing returns can magnify this advantage and the product or company or technology can go on to lock in the market.

Three basic reasons are suggested by Arthur for increasing returns to occur: (1) high upfront (fixed) costs and very low variable costs; (2) network effects, that is, the value of a product increases with the number of other users of that product, and (3) 'customer groove-in' or high switching costs. Knowledge-intensive products such as software have all these characteristics. Raw-material-intensive products such as bulk chemicals have none of them.

The logic of increasing returns has become an important concept in economics, and it has massive implications for the world of business. As argued by Arthur (ibid.: 101), 'the two worlds (traditional business, knowledge-intensive business) have different economics. They differ in behaviour, style and culture. They call for different management techniques, strategies and codes of government regulation.'

What does this have to do with entrepreneurship in MNCs? The argument is that the two different models of entrepreneurship can be mapped quite clearly onto the two different economic logics. Consider Figure 5.1, which plots the 39 initiatives studied during the author's doctoral research in terms of the internal–external split and the industrial sector. The result is quite striking: internal initiatives are found exclusively in capital-intensive manufacturing firms, that is, those in which diminishing returns still apply. External initiatives, in contrast, are far more common in high-technology firms, in which increasing returns are more likely. Of course the limited scope of this data means that it proves nothing, but the apparent relationship is sufficiently clear for it to be worth exploring as a hypothesis.

The argument, then, is that Kirznerian entrepreneurship is about fine-tuning an existing system, which would appear to be more relevant in the diminishing returns world. Schumpeterian entrepreneurship is about identifying and acting on new opportunities, which is more consistent with the logic of increasing returns. Figure 5.2 illustrates this logic, and the following paragraphs explain it in greater depth.

	Internal initiative	External initiative
Diminishing returns sector (manufacturing in 3M, Monsanto, Honeywell controls)	17	0
Increasing returns sector (Hewlett Packard, Amazon computer systems, Honeywell industrial control systems)	5	17

Figure 5.1 *Cross-tabulation of initiative type and industry sector (Source: Birkinshaw, 1995, 1997)*

Conditions for Kirznerian entrepreneurship

Successful firms in the world of diminishing returns are good at managing their resources in an efficient manner. The emphasis is typically on efficiency, high quality and cost control. Such a business environment works best with a traditional hierarchical model, one in which the top management have a firm grip on expenditure and on the inputs and outputs of the system. The emphasis is on the exploitation of existing assets rather than the exploration of new ones (March, 1991).

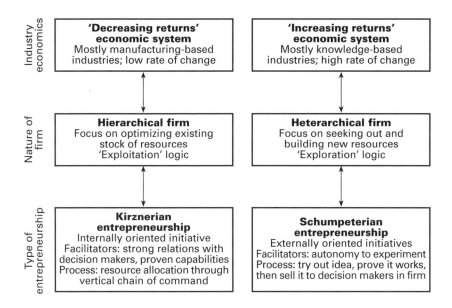

Figure 5.2 *Models of entrepreneurship and industry economics*

Is there a role for entrepreneurship in this sort of system? Not in the traditional sense of entrepreneurship as a Schumpeterian process, but if one adopts the Kirznerian logic of entrepreneurship pushing a system towards its equilibrium position, then it is entirely appropriate. Entrepreneurship of this form is therefore internally focused. It is directed towards opportunities to improve the allocation of resources inside the firm, by reconfiguring existing assets and decreasing the X-inefficiency of the firm. The entrepreneurial process follows the traditional model whereby the idea is put forward and builds impetus through the vertical chain of command. Key success factors for would-be entrepreneurs are good relationships with decision makers at head office and proven capabilities in the relevant areas.

This is a summary of the internal initiatives discussed in Chapters 2 to 4. It is also interesting to note that such initiatives have almost exclusively occurred in traditional manufacturing industries such as chemicals and industrial products.

Conditions for Schumpeterian entrepreneurship

The world of increasing returns requires a very different approach. Firms in increasing returns industries are aware of the rapid rate of change in their environment, and the importance of being a first-mover in new business areas. As a result they devote most of their effort to exploring new opportunities, rather than exploiting existing ones. Arthur (1996) refers to this as the search for the 'next big thing'.

What is the appropriate organization for this sort of strategy? Hedlund (1986) proposes the term 'heterarchy' as an alternative to hierarchy. Heterarchy implies flexibility, greater decision-making autonomy among subsidiaries and continuous adaptation to environmental change. All these traits are appropriate in an increasing-returns environment in which the firm is seeking out and building on new opportunities wherever in the world they transpire. Much the same logic was offered by Arthur (1996: 104).

> In this milieu, management becomes not production oriented but mission oriented. Hierarchies flatten . . . because to be effective the deliverers of the next thing for the company need to be organized like commando units in small teams that report directly to the CEO. Such people need free rein.

Both Hedlund's and Arthur's organizational models suggest a very important role for entrepreneurship in the Schumpeterian sense. If the goal of the firm is to seek out the 'next big thing' and throw resources at it quickly, then the structure needs to be much flatter, with far greater autonomy for operating units than in a traditional hierarchical firm. And these units also have to be very entrepreneurial, on the lookout for new business ideas that could revolutionize the firm's strategy. Entrepreneurship of this type therefore has to be externally oriented. The process is geared towards trying out new ideas in their business context first, and only later seeking approval and legitimacy from the head office.

This represents a summary of the external initiative process described in the previous three chapters. The three examples described above – NCR, Ericsson and HP – are all cases where the logic of increasing returns applies: where the upfront development costs are huge, the network economies are significant and there are significant switching costs between competing products.

Conclusion

This chapter has sought to reconcile the empirical material in Chapters 2 to 4 with the literature on entrepreneurship, or more specifically the theories of Schumpeter and Kirzner. The logic that internally oriented initiatives are basically Kirznerian while externally oriented initiatives are more Schumpeterian, may seem unduly simple but it captures the basic differences between the two. It also suggests a number of implications in terms of the economic systems in which the two forms of initiative are likely to transpire. Kirznerian initiatives are more suitable in the efficiency-dominated world of diminishing returns. Schumpeterian initiatives are more appropriate for knowledge-intensive industries in which the objective is to search out the 'next big thing' rather than optimize the existing stock of assets.

This completes the discussion of entrepreneurship. The next chapters will move on to other theoretical angles, such as the theory of the firm and the resource-based perspective. Chapter 8 will revisit some of these ideas in the discussion of the internal market model of the multinational firm.

Key ideas in Chapter 5

- There are two different ways of viewing entrepreneurship in economic theory. Schumpeter's view of entrepreneurship is a process of creative destruction in which the entrepreneur pushes the economic system *out of* equilibrium. Kirzner, in contrast, models entrepreneurship as an ongoing process of adjustment *towards* equilibrium.
- The two basic forms of subsidiary initiative parallel the two forms of entrepreneurship. Externally oriented initiatives are analogous to Schumpeterian entrepreneurship because they push the MNC towards new products and markets. Internally oriented initiatives are analogous to Kirznerian entrepreneurship because they represent a way of streamlining the internal network of activities.

(continued)

- There is some evidence that the relative importance of these two forms of initiative varies by industry. Internally oriented initiatives appear to be more prevalent in traditional 'diminishing returns' industries such as chemicals and automobiles, while externally oriented initiatives are seen more often in 'increasing returns' industries such as software and telecommunications.

Notes

1   See Jacobson (1992) for a review of the Austrian literature as it applies to strategic management.

2   Of course MNCs are not concerned only with efficiency. An important counterweight is local responsiveness, in terms of adapting products to local customer needs and being sensitive to local government demands. Such factors will obviously constrain the resource allocation decision.

3   It is worth exploring in greater detail the question of internal resource allocation efficiency. Consider a typical multinational firm with manufacturing operations in half a dozen countries, how can this set of operations be made more efficient? Two approaches can be envisaged:

- Resources can be reconfigured, so that each plant focuses on what it does best. Perhaps the German plant focuses on customized engineering work, while the Czech plant does the high-volume assembly. This is aimed at reducing inefficiencies in resource allocation within the firm.
- Resources can be left in the same place, but the operating practices in each plant are compared and the 'best practices' are then applied to those plants that are lagging behind. This reduces X-inefficiency in the firm.

Both of these approaches are valuable, of course, but they operate in distinctly different ways. From my reading of Leibenstein (1966), his focus is on the latter process, whereas the focus in this chapter is on the former. But there is also substantial overlap between the two. Just as initiative can be a valuable driver of internal resource-allocation efficiency, it can also be an important spur to greater X-efficiency. As Leibenstein himself notes in a separate paper (1968), 'there is a significant relation between the entrepreneur's perceptive capacity and the fact that firms operate under some degree of slack'. Hence there are many examples of subsidiary units developing best practices, which are then taken up by other units around the world. Equally there are many examples of subsidiary units proactively going out into their network of affiliates around the world to seek out new ways of doing things.

6

Mapping the Process of Subsidiary Evolution

This chapter, and those that follow it, take an increasingly broad focus. Up to now the emphasis has been on subsidiary initiative and its specific effects on various subsidiary and firm-level phenomena. The relative emphasis is now reversed – the focus is on a better understanding of certain subsidiary and firm-level issues, and the role of subsidiary initiative as one of several processes that affects them.

The specific objective of this chapter is to model the process of subsidiary evolution[1] that was hinted at in Chapter 4. Subsidiary evolution can be defined for the moment as the result of an accumulation or depletion of capabilities over time. While not forgetting that our focus on the subsidiary, rather than the MNC as a whole, makes this approach somewhat unconventional, the definition is still remarkably consistent with the established body of literature referred to as the 'dynamic capabilities perspective'. This literature can be traced back to Penrose's (1959) *Theory of the Growth of the Firm*, and includes important contributions from Teece et al. (1997), Kogut and Zander (1992), Nelson and Winter (1982) and Dierickx and Cool (1989). The dynamic capabilities perspective is broadly concerned with the 'mechanisms by which firms accumulate and dissipate new skills and capabilities' (Teece et al., 1997).

Factors determining subsidiary evolution

What factors determine the evolution of the subsidiary? The argument developed so far in this book is that evolution is organic, in that it is driven from within by the specific initiatives of subsidiary managers and the propagation of organizational routines that have emerged over time. But it is also strongly influenced by outside factors, notably the actions taken by parent company managers and the constraints imposed by the environment in which it is located. Subsidiary evolution, in other words, is a function of head office assignment, subsidiary choice and environmental determinism, the same set of contextual factors discussed in Chapter 4 as the determinants of initiative. Let us briefly consider each.

Head office assignment

Much of the traditional literature on the multinational firm sees the evolution of the subsidiary as a function of decisions made by head office managers. In Vernon's (1966) product life cycle model, for example, the subsidiary moves from being a reseller of goods made in the home market, to a low-cost producer for the local market, to a supplier of high-quality goods to the home market and other countries. Equally, in the internationalization process model of Johanson and Vahlne (1977), increasing commitment in the foreign market is a head office decision based on the experiential knowledge of operating in that market. In both cases the subsidiary goes through a process of resource accumulation, but entirely on the basis of decisions made by head office managers.

Subsidiary choice

The subsidiary choice perspective needs no introduction as it has been described and referred to throughout this book. Rather than assuming that the subsidiary is an instrument of the parent company, it recognizes that the subsidiary often controls valuable resources and vital relationships with local actors that lessen its dependency on the parent company. This gives the subsidiary some degree of freedom in choosing how to conduct itself, leaving open the possibility of undertaking initiatives that are not formally sanctioned by the parent company. The degree to which the subsidiary is able to act autonomously is a function of many factors, such as distance from head office, access to resources, and network relationships. And as observed earlier, the extent to which such autonomous action is condoned by the parent company also varies enormously.

Local environment determinism

Much of the mainstream organization theory literature views organizational action as constrained or determined by the environment in which it occurs (Hannan and Freeman, 1977; Meyer and Rowan, 1977; Pfeffer and Salancik, 1978). Researchers on the MNC have adapted this perspective by proposing that each subsidiary operates in its own unique task environment, which constrains or determines the activities of that subsidiary (Ghoshal and Bartlett, 1990; Ghoshal and Nohria, 1989; Rosenzweig and Singh, 1991; Westney, 1994). The argument, in essence, is that each subsidiary operates under a unique set of conditions to which it has to adapt in order to be effective. The nature of the local environment, as defined by customers, competitors, suppliers and government bodies, thus has an important influence on the activities undertaken by the subsidiary.

The process of subsidiary evolution

Subsidiary evolution is therefore driven by the interaction of these three factors. But this does not tell the whole story, because the underlying processes of evolution are not specified. To make sense of these, it is necessary to draw on the dynamic capabilities perspective and a number of related bodies of literature.

Let us begin with a few definitions. *Resources* are the stock of available factors owned or controlled by the subsidiary, and *capabilities* are a subsidiary's capacity to deploy resources, usually in combination, using organizational processes to bring about a desired end (Amit and Schoemaker, 1993). Subsidiary capabilities can be specific to a functional area, for example flexible production, research into fibre optics or logistics management, or they can be more broadly based, for example total quality management, systems integration, innovation or government relations.

Subsidiary evolution is the result of an accumulation or depletion of capabilities over time. To some extent capabilities are accumulated through organizational routines (Nelson and Winter, 1982) that have emerged over time, but the process can also be strongly influenced by various subsidiary, corporate and local environmental factors, many of which were discussed earlier.

An important point to underscore here is that the subsidiary's capabilities are to some extent distinct from the capabilities of the headquarters and its sister subsidiaries. In other words, the particular geographical setting and history of the subsidiary are responsible for defining a development path that is absolutely unique to that subsidiary, which in turn results in a profile of capabilities that is in turn unique (Teece et al., 1997). There are also, of course, shared capabilities between subsidiaries, such as those codified in company manuals or blueprints. The evidence, however, indicates that the transfer of capabilities between units of the same firm is far from trivial, and is a function of the codifiability of the capability in question (Zander, 1994), the motivations of the receiving units and a host of contextual variables (Szulanski, 1996). Capabilities, simply stated, are 'sticky', and cannot be easily transferred from one subsidiary to the next even when transfer is undertaken willingly.

Related to the stickiness of subsidiary capabilities is their path dependence. Capabilities are not easily transferred or readily dissipated. They develop over time as a result of past experiences and are subsequently applied to new or related areas of business. To some extent new capabilities are always being developed, but they typically emerge at the margin of existing capabilities in response to competitive demands (see below). As a result it is possible to think in terms of path-dependent trajectories of capabilities that gradually evolve over time. Large-scale grafting of new capabilities onto the subsidiary's existing stock of capabilities can be achieved through merger or acquisition, but such a process is often problematic because it inevitably involves transfer and/or combination (Huber, 1991; Madhok, 1997).

The visible manifestation of the subsidiary's role in the MNC is its *charter*, defined as the business, or elements of the business, in which the subsidiary participates, and for which it is recognized to have responsibility within the MNC (Galunic and Eisenhardt, 1996). Charter can thus be defined in terms of markets served, products manufactured, technologies held, functional areas covered or any combination thereof. The charter is typically a shared understanding between the subsidiary and the HQ regarding the subsidiary's responsibilities.

The relationship between the subsidiary's charter and its underlying capabilities is not a simple one. In the case where the subsidiary's charter does not change for a long period of time, the management of the subsidiary are likely to steer resource deployment and capability-accumulation efforts towards the fulfilment of that charter, so that eventually the subsidiary's capability profile is a reflection of its charter. However, if there is a high degree of change in the subsidiary's resource base (for example through merger and acquisition), its charter or the markets that the charter is directed towards, then at any given point in time there are likely to be mismatches between the subsidiary's capability profile and its official charter. The point, which will be elaborated further in the next section, is simply that the *concept of subsidiary evolution must take into account both the charter of the subsidiary and its underlying capabilities*. It is wrong to assume that the two simply move together.

One final line of reasoning regarding subsidiary charters and capabilities needs to be mentioned here, namely *that in most MNCs there is internal competition for charters*. This competition is both for existing charters (where one subsidiary 'steals' a charter from another) and for new charters (where two or more subsidiaries 'bid' against one another). The best evidence for internal charter competition is provided by Galunic and Eisenhardt (1996) and Galunic (1996), who have studied the processes through which divisions of the Omni corporation gained and lost charters from one another. Charter competition is also mentioned in a number of studies of Canadian subsidiaries (Birkinshaw, 1996; Crookell, 1986; White and Poynter, 1984).

The idea that charters might shift from one subsidiary to another appears strange at first sight, given the argument above that each subsidiary has a unique capability profile. However in many cases subsidiaries have similar, though not identical, capability profiles. Take for example the case of a large silicon chip manufacturer, which will typically have ten or more fabrication plants at various sites around the world. These plants all have the basic capability to manufacture chips, but at the same time they do so with rather different technologies and different levels of quality control, cost, process enhancement and so on. In all these plants there is an ongoing process of internal benchmarking and capability upgrading because a new investment can potentially be made at any one of the existing plants.

Not all charters are 'contestable' in this fashion. Some charters are country-specific so they are linked inextricably to the local subsidiary operation; others are tied to large immobile assets (for example an automobile plant) so they cannot easily be shifted to another location. Many more, however, are readily contestable, especially when the underlying resources upon which they are based are mobile. It is, then, the latent mobility of charters and the competition between subsidiary units for charters that is one of the fundamental drivers of the subsidiary evolution process.

The importance of internal competition for charters can be shown in another way. Porter's (1980, 1990) thinking on competitive advantage suggests that it is exposure to demanding customers, leading-edge competitors and high-quality suppliers that forces firms to upgrade their capabilities. In the case of the subsidiary company, one can identify a competitive environment with both external and internal components: the external elements are customers, competitors and suppliers in the local environment; the internal elements are other corporate units that buy from or sell to the 'focal' subsidiary, and sister subsidiaries that are competing for new and existing charters. The argument is that internal competitive forces – when they are released – are as critical to the capability enhancement process as external competitive forces. In some MNCs there is no internal competitive environment, because all sourcing relationships and charter allocations are centrally planned by head office managers, but increasingly firms are making use of internal market mechanisms to foster the competitive dynamics described here (Halal, 1994).

In summary, subsidiary evolution is defined in terms of (1) *the enhancement/atrophy of capabilities in the subsidiary* and (2) *the establishment/loss of the commensurate charter*. Subsidiary development consists of capability enhancement and charter establishment; subsidiary decline consists of capability atrophy and charter loss. Capability change may lead or follow the change in the commensurate charter, but for evolution to have occurred the charter must eventually reflect the underlying capabilities of the subsidiary. Note that this definition deliberately excludes self-serving or empire-building behaviour, whereby the subsidiary develops capabilities that are *not* aligned with the strategic priorities of the MNC. The argument is that the process of assigning a charter to the subsidiary is explicit acknowledgement by the corporate management that the underlying capabilities are valued. If the capabilities are not valued there is no charter change, and evolution has not occurred.

Generic subsidiary evolution processes

The phenomenon of subsidiary evolution will now be reconsidered using the theoretical ideas developed above. The idea here is to put forward five generic processes, or types of subsidiary evolution, and to use the theoretical insights indicated above and in the earlier part of the chapter to propose a series of causal relationships linking certain contextual factors to each of the five processes.

Figure 6.1 shows the possible combinations of capability change and charter change in the subsidiary. As noted earlier, it seems extremely unlikely that the subsidiary's charter will exactly mirror the subsidiary's capability profile. Instead the capability change will either lead or follow the charter change. Type A is the situation in which charter change leads subsequently to a change in the subsidiary's capability profile. Given that charter assignment is the parent company's responsibility and that the capabilities are not already in existence, this process is designated as *parent-driven investment*. While the subsidiary's management may have some influence over the process (notably through high performance), they are typically actively competing for the charter with other subsidiaries, so the development of the commensurate capabilities begins only once the charter has been assigned. Type B is the situation in which capability enhancement leads subsequently to a change in the subsidiary's charter. In essence it represents a strategic move by the subsidiary's management, who see the opportunity to gain a new or enhanced charter if they can demonstrate that they have the necessary capabilities (as described in Chapter 2). However, charter change in this case is not guaranteed, for example if the capabilities in question are not deemed by the corporate management to be valuable. This process can be designated as *subsidiary-driven charter extension*. Types D and E are the reverse of types A and B. Type D is the case of *parent-driven divestment*, where the subsidiary loses its charter for a certain product, technology or market and the commensurate capabilities gradually atrophy. Type E is the case of *atrophy through subsidiary neglect*, where the subsidiary's capabilities gradually wither away over time, its performance (for that charter) suffers and eventually the parent company takes away the charter. Finally, type C is *subsidiary-driven charter strengthening*, whereby the subsidiary sharpens or strengthens its existing capabilities and maintains its charter. It could be argued that this is not a pure case of subsidiary evolution, but it is included to cater for the situation in which the subsidiary opts to deepen its capabilities in one specific area (that is, its current charter) rather than seek out new charters. As part of a long-term strategy of subsidiary development, charter strengthening is probably an important phase for the subsidiary to go through because it ensures that it has leading-edge capabilities *vis-à-vis* both internal and external competitors. Note, however, that in such a case it is harder (though not

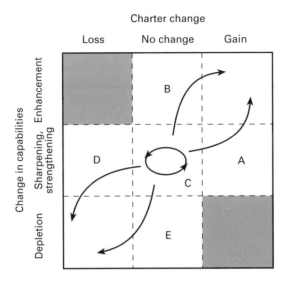

Figure 6.1 *Subsidiary evolution as a function of capability and charter change*

impossible) to identify when evolution has occurred because the charter is maintained rather than enhanced.

One further observation should be made at this stage. Each process represents a discrete phase that experience tells us may take anything from a few weeks to a few years to complete. Over a longer period one would expect to see multiple phases of development, including positive and negative steps as well as subsidiary- and parent-driven ones. The unit of analysis under investigation here is thus the single period that is focused on one charter change and a change in the commensurate capabilities. Subsidiary evolution, broadly conceived, can also refer to aggregate changes over time (as described in Chapter 4), but for the sake of conceptual and operational clarity it is necessary to work at the lower level of analysis.

Two questions follow from the categorization in Figure 6.1. First, what do these five processes look like (in terms of action–outcome relationships)? And second, what specific contextual factors are responsible for promoting or suppressing them? The remainder of the chapter addresses these two questions, using Table 6.1 as a framework.

The five generic processes

Type A: parent-driven investment. The parent-driven investment process consists of one clearly defined event, that is, the decision to enhance

Table 6.1   *Five generic subsidiary evolution processes*

Contextual factors	Action	Outcome
Parent-company factors • Competitive internal resource allocation • Decentralization of decision making • Ethnocentrism of parent management	**(A) Parent-driven investment** *Parent:* Decision to make investment, evaluation of various locations *Subsidiary:* Lobbying →	Establishment of new charter in subsidiary; gradual development of commensurate capabilities
Subsidiary factors • Track record of subsidiary • Credibility of subsidiary management	**(B) Subsidiary-driven charter enhancement** *Subsidiary:* Identification of new opportunities, building capabilities, proposal to parent *Parent:* Judgement on subsidiary proposal →	Extension of charter in subsidiary
• Entrepreneurial orientation of subsidiary employees • Contestability of subsidiary existing charter	**(C) Subsidiary-driven charter strengthening** *Subsidiary:* Competitiveness-driven search, upgrading of existing capabilities →	Strengthening of existing charter in subsidiary
Host country factors • Strategic importance of country • Host government support • Relative cost of factor inputs	**(D) Parent-driven divestment** *Parent:* Decision to divest, evaluation of various locations *Subsidiary:* Lobbying → **(E) Atrophy through subsidiary neglect**	Loss or diminution of charter in subsidiary, atrophy of existing capabilities
• Dynamism of local business environment	*Subsidiary:* Inaction, atrophy of capabilities *Parent:* Judgement on subsidiary's lack of competitiveness →	Loss or diminution of charter in subsidiary

the subsidiary's charter, preceded by a period of negotiation and deliberation by the parent company and the subsidiary, and followed by a period of capability development by the subsidiary in order satisfactorily to deliver on the new charter. The action taken by the parent company management is typically an evaluation of the relative merits of various locations for the planned investment, followed by the decision to make the charter change in the subsidiary. The action taken by the subsidiary's management will vary enormously, but it typically consists of lobbying parent company managers to decide in their favour. In most cases the process will involve the commitment of considerable resources to the subsidiary, for example through the establishment of a new factory or the creation of a research and development group. However it is also possible that the decision will simply be one of charter change in the subsidiary, for example the extension of market responsibility from the UK to Europe.

As discussed in Chapter 2, the process is driven by the parent company's desire to select, according to whatever criteria they deem appropriate, the optimum location for a new investment. Some MNCs use a formalized request-for-proposal procedure in such cases, whereby proposed corporate-level investments are opened up to all interested subsidiary operations and allocated on the basis of the bids that are received. In other cases the process is less structured, and may involve a variety of informal decision-making procedures. In both cases there is at least implicit competition between locations for the new investment, which typically leads to active lobbying by various subsidiaries and host governments.

Type B: subsidiary-driven charter extension. This is, of course, the subsidiary initiative that was described at length in Chapters 2 and 3. It involves a long and often slow process of capability building followed by an extension to the subsidiary's charter. The process represents a conscious effort by the subsidiary management to seek out and develop new business opportunities, and then put them forward to parent company managers. On the assumption that parent company managers are inherently risk averse in their decisions about which subsidiaries should have responsibility for which charters, the logic here is that the subsidiary management build up the required capabilities first, and only seek charter extension once they can demonstrate those capabilities.

In the current context, the process involves three distinct steps by subsidiary managers. First, an initiative-driven search for new market opportunities in both the subsidiary's local market and within the corporate system. Second, the pursuit of a specific market opportunity, and the development of the appropriate capabilities to fulfil it. Third, a proposal to the parent company that the subsidiary's charter be enhanced. For the parent company, the only action required is a judgement on whether to grant the subsidiary its requested charter enhancement. In the case of internal initiatives, they will typically be informed of the subsidiary's initiative throughout the process, whereas most external initiatives will be deliberately pursued by subsidiary managers without the knowledge of the parent company (see Chapter 3). In all situations, though, the subsidiary-driven charter enhancement process can be seen as fairly 'political', in that it relies to a great degree on the subsidiary-level champion gaining support at head office through his or her personal contacts.

Type C: subsidiary-driven charter strengthening. As with the previous process, this case is driven entirely by the initiative of subsidiary managers. It is triggered by concerns about the subsidiary's competitiveness, *vis-à-vis* both sister subsidiaries and external competitors. The competitors provide specific cues to subsidiary management regarding their relative strengths and weaknesses, which leads to attempts to enhance the relevant set of capabilities. This process may or may not also involve external benchmarking and internal transfers of best practice. The net results, assuming the process has been effective, are lower costs and/or quality and service improvements, and thus a strengthening of the subsidiary's existing charter. There may be no head office involvement in this process *per se*, given that no official change to the charter is being suggested, but the capability strengthening process will lead to a stronger subsidiary performance and thus an enhanced level of credibility and visibility *vis-à-vis* head office managers.

Type D: parent-driven divestment. The process of parent-driven divestment is the mirror image of the first (parent-driven investment). The typical scenario, as discussed briefly in Chapter 5, is that the parent company has made a decision to rationalize its international operations and/or to exit certain businesses, but the decision about *which* ones to divest has not been finalized. Such a scenario can be triggered by a need to cut costs or by the desire for greater strategic focus on core activities. The fate of the subsidiary may thus be closure, sale to another company or spin-off as a separate entity.

The evaluation process is influenced by a host of factors, including the existing capabilities of the subsidiary relative to others, and the attractiveness of the host-country market according to a number of criteria. Subsidiary managers and host-country governments will sometimes have the opportunity to lobby against closure, but more often the decision will be presented as a *fait accompli* by the parent company management.

The final decision results in a charter loss for the focal subsidiary. This may include the sale or closure of all associated activities, for example when a plant is shut down. In such a case the subsidiary's capabilities are lost at the same time. Equally likely is the case where a charter is lost but the subsidiary as a whole continues to exist (Galunic and Eisenhardt, 1996). In such a case the capabilities that were associated with the old charter will be gradually lost as employees are reassigned to new roles and develop new skills. However it is possible that the remaining capabilities are actually redeployed for the development of a new charter, that is, in a type B subsidiary-driven extension process. This process has been labelled charter renewal (Birkinshaw, 1996).

Type E: atrophy through subsidiary neglect. The final case is one in which the subsidiary's capabilities gradually atrophy while the charter is retained. The argument here is the reverse of that put forward for types B and C. Essentially the subsidiary management's *lack of attention* can be seen as the driver of this process. The subsidiary becomes less and less competitive over time. This can be simply a case of poor management, but it is more likely to stem from a lack of competition. If, for example, the subsidiary has guaranteed internal contracts for its products and the corporation as a whole is making money, the pressure to reduce costs or improve service is likely to be low.

The subsidiary continues to fulfil its charter, but on the basis of capabilities that are not leading-edge and that gradually atrophy over time through lack of attention. Eventually this situation comes to the attention of head office managers, either because it is negatively affecting the competitiveness of the entire MNC or because internal performance measures reveal the below-par performance of the focal subsidiary. Depending on the urgency of the change that is demanded of head-office managers, the subsidiary may be given the opportunity to turn things around, or it may lose its charter immediately.[2] Another scenario, given the discussion about type C (charter strengthening), is that the subsidiary is doing a satisfactory job of maintaining its capabilities, but when faced with a global rationalization programme it becomes apparent that other subsidiaries have upgraded their capabilities more effectively. Charter loss follows, simply because the focal subsidiary's capabilities are weaker than those of its sister subsidiaries. Atrophy, in this sense, refers to the level of the capabilities relative to other subsidiaries, rather than in an absolute sense.

Contextual factors impacting the generic processes

Having described the five generic processes it is worth briefly revisiting the contextual factors that influence their occurrence. The three-fold categorization introduced earlier will be retained, and within each category a number of different factors will be identified.

Head office assignment

The concept of head office assignment can now be broadened, in the light of the earlier discussion about internal competition, to include all those factors that come under the direct control of head office managers. These include the following:

- *Use of competitive internal resource allocation systems.* Some firms actively use systems that promote internal competition, either by requesting bids for new investments or by creating a system through which existing charters can be 'challenged' by other units. Such a system has substantial implications for subsidiary evolution because it legitimizes a process by which subsidiaries can both gain and lose charters. In its absence, by contrast, resource-allocation decisions are made with extreme bounded rationality, which typically means favouring investment locations with which the decision makers are familiar, that is, the home country.
- *Decentralization of decision making.* Researchers on MNCs have given a lot of attention to the issue of decentralization or autonomy in subsidiaries, both as a cause and as a consequence of certain behaviours and operational characteristics in subsidiaries (for example Gates and Egelhoff, 1986; Prahalad and Doz, 1981). The expectation is that decentralized decision making will favour the processes of subsidiary-driven charter enhancement and strengthening, while it will have no substantial impact on parent-driven investment.
- *Ethnocentrism on the part of the parent-company management.* This concept was discussed in Chapter 3. The logic is that a high level of ethnocentrism will negatively affect the likelihood of significant investments being made outside the firm's home country. This logic would be expected to hold not only for subsidiary-driven charter enhancement but also for the parent-driven investment process, because many such investments can potentially be made in the home country.

Subsidiary choice

Subsidiary choice includes all things that are under the direct control of subsidiary management. Building on the discussion in Chapter 2 and above, the following factors are important:

- *Subsidiary track record.* The most critical factor affecting subsidiary evolution is the extent to which it has delivered, over the years, results that meet or exceed the expectations of the parent company. Even if one adopts a political perspective on decision making, the track record of the subsidiary remains of central importance, because it provides the justification for a corporate manager's decision to enhance or reduce the subsidiary's charter. Only the subsidiary-driven charter strengthening process is likely to be unaffected by the subsidiary's track record, because it occurs without parent company involvement.

- *Quality of the subsidiary–parent relationship.* This refers to the informal ties between senior managers in the subsidiary and key decision makers in the parent company. Often subsidiary managers are expatriates or people who have spent a period at head office, and have therefore built up a strong network of personal relationships with parent company managers. Such networks represent a social control system, which can be an effective means of holding the firm together. The quality of subsidiary–parent relationships will have a very strong effect on the subsidiary-driven charter enhancement process because it is entrepreneurial in nature. Equally, the quality of subsidiary–parent relationships will reduce the likelihood of subsidiary decline, just because the parent company's decisions in such situations are in part politically determined.
- *Entrepreneurial orientation of subsidiary employees.* This refers to the predisposition of employees throughout the subsidiary to be alert and responsive to new opportunities. As already discussed, both the subsidiary-driven charter enhancement process and the subsidiary-driven charter strengthening process will be positively affected by the entrepreneurial orientation of subsidiary employees, while atrophy through subsidiary neglect will be negatively affected.
- *Contestability of the subsidiary's existing charter.* Because each subsidiary has a distinct, although often overlapping, set of capabilities *vis-à-vis* other subsidiaries, the contestability of an existing charter (that is, the extent to which other subsidiaries can potentially take it on) will have a significant impact on the subsidiary evolution process. Most obviously, charter contestability is likely to lead to a subsidiary-driven charter strengthening process, because managers are aware that they can lose their charter to other subsidiaries if it is not competitive. By the same logic, charter contestability also reduces the likelihood of atrophy through subsidiary neglect.

Local environment determinism

All of the processes are to some extent affected by conditions in the local market system. Such factors may play a more passive role than those that occur through head office assignment or subsidiary choice, but they are present nonetheless.

- *Dynamism of the local business environment.* This refers to the extent and quality of the interaction between competing and complementary firms in industry clusters, as described in Porter's (1990) diamond framework. The argument is that a dynamic local business environment provides the stimuli for upgrading the subsidiary's capabilities in much the same way that internal competition does. As a result, subsidiary-driven charter enhancement and strengthening processes will be positively affected by local dynamism, whereas atrophy through subsidiary neglect is likely to occur through a *lack* of local dynamism.

- *Host-government support.* This is still a very important factor. Even in today's almost-free-trade world host governments are still able to offer direct financial incentives for foreign investment, as well as a host of indirect incentives, such as soft loans, personnel training and infra-structural support. In addition, host-government agencies can help MNCs to identify and evaluate potential sites and introduce pro-spective partners. Host-government support can affect all five proc-esses. It will typically have a strong positive effect in cases of parent-driven investment. It will have an equally strong but negative effect in cases of subsidiary decline, in that government representa-tives will lobby hard with the MNC to reverse or modify the decision to divest a subsidiary.
- *Strategic importance of the country to the MNC.* This is obviously an important factor in the parent-driven investment decision, and in the parallel decision to divest. However subsidiary-driven charter enhancement and charter strengthening will not be substantially affected by this factor, in that they represent bets on the subsidiary and its existing capabilities, and not on the country *per se.*
- *Relative cost of factor inputs in the country.* This factor parallels the previous one, but in the reverse direction. Thus if a market has relatively high factor input costs it becomes *ceteris paribus* a less attractive location for a parent-driven investment and a more attrac-tive candidate for divestment.

Concluding observations

This chapter represents a broadening of our outlook from a focus on the process of subsidiary initiative to a consideration of the evolution of the subsidiary as a whole, which is driven in part by subsidiary initiative, and in part by a number of corporate and environmental factors.

The primary insight from this chapter is that the evolution of the subsidiary can be modelled in a way that parallels Penrose's *Theory of the Growth of the Firm* (1959), and the dynamic capabilities perspective in general. Evolution, according to this perspective, is driven fundamentally from within as a function of the capabilities that have accumulated in the subsidiary. Or in the words of Penrose (ibid.: 56) 'The very processes of operation and of expansion are intimately associated with a process by which knowledge is increased.' The major modification that is necessary when looking at a subsidiary unit is that growth has to be sanctioned by the parent company. Thus the concept of a 'charter' was introduced as a means of separating out growth that is valued by the rest of the MNC from growth that is self-serving (and thus destructive). A distinction was also made between cases of growth that are 'decreed' by the parent company and cases of growth that are built from within.

This is not, however, the whole story. The dynamic capabilities perspective, like other theoretical perspectives on strategy, is ultimately concerned with the creation of firm-level competitive advantage (Teece et al., 1997). While this chapter has shown how subsidiaries develop new capabilities and charters, it has not explicitly linked this process of evolution to the competitiveness of the MNC as a whole. This is a separate problem, and one which is addressed in the next chapter.

Key ideas in Chapter 6

- Subsidiary evolution refers to the process in which the subsidiary's capabilities and charter change over time. The inclusion of 'charter' is vital to this definition – some subsidiaries will develop new capabilities, but unless they are reflected in enhancement of the official charter of the subsidiary they are effectively wasted.
- Subsidiary evolution is a function of subsidiary initiative, HQ investment decisions and opportunities in the local environment. Five generic processes can be identified: (1) subsidiary-driven charter enhancement; (2) parent-driven investment; (3) atrophy through subsidiary neglect; (4) parent-driven divestment; and (5) subsidiary-driven charter strengthening. The first two are positive, the second two are negative and the third is neutral.
- The process of subsidiary evolution is analogous to Penrose's (1959) theory of the growth of the firm. In fact the MNC subsidiary represents a more general case than the stand-alone firm, because the constraints on growth are imposed by the parent company as well as by the firm's resource base.

Notes

1   The word evolution is used here rather than development (as used in Chapter 4) because development implies a positive cycle of growth and the accumulation of resources, whereas evolution implies a broader notion of change in a positive or negative direction. Thus to make the ideas here more generalizable, evolution is the appropriate term.

2   Frequently the charter loss process is rather more gradual than this, in that the subsidiary finds itself with increasingly unimportant charters.

7

Perspectives on the Theory of the Multinational Corporation

The purpose of this chapter is to look at the various theoretical perspectives on the MNC, and to see what implications the ideas presented in this book have for them. This is a far from simple task. The first challenge is to be clear about the meaning of the 'theory of the multinational corporation'. Most academics would immediately acknowledge the transaction-cost-based theory of international production that began with Hymer (1960/1976) and was subsequently developed by Buckley and Casson (1976), Rugman (1981), Dunning (1980, 1988) and others. Others would also accept that a network theory of the MNC has emerged in recent years, through the research of Hedlund (1986), Ghoshal and Bartlett (1990), Forsgren and Johanson (1992) and others. There is also a good argument to be made that the currently popular resource-based view of the firm (Barney, 1991; Connor, 1991; Penrose, 1959; Wernerfelt, 1984) should have some implications for the MNC, even though those implications have yet to be spelled out. In this chapter all three of these theoretical perspectives are addressed.

There is a second challenge in writing this chapter, namely that the implications of the ideas presented in this book for the three theories are likely to be very different. Using the age-old concept of falsifiability (Popper, 1968), an obvious first line of attack is to ask whether the theory in question is consistent with what has been observed. If the empirical observations cannot be reconciled with the theory, then it follows that there are limitations to the theory and it has to be adapted.

But the criterion of falsifiability, as it turns out, reveals the weakness of much of the so-called theory referred to above. The network theory of the MNC, in particular, appears to be unfalsifiable. It is a good way of describing the MNC, and it allows one to create a lot of testable hypotheses at the level of individual relationships, but in its current form it probably deserves to be called a paradigm or framework rather than a theory. To a lesser degree, one can also level the same criticism at the other two theories mentioned above.

Table 7.1 provides a much-simplified synopsis of the three theories, and the extent to which the ideas presented in this book are consistent with or relevant to these theories. The point of this table is to show that the agenda when discussing each theory is very different. For the transaction cost theory of international production, the important issue is to show how subsidiary-driven initiative can help the MNC to build firm-specific or location-specific advantages. For the resource-based view of the firm, the key question is how resources and capabilities developed at the level of the subsidiary unit can result in competitive advantage at the MNC level. And for the network theory of the MNC, the challenge lies in extending or developing the theory in the light of the ideas presented here. Each will be considered in turn.

The transaction-cost theory of international production

As stated by Dunning (1993), the purpose of the transaction-cost theory of international production is to 'explain the level and pattern of the foreign value-added activities of firms'. This involves an understanding of the original decision to invest internationally, but also an understanding of how international activities have subsequently been configured. It centres on the insight that imperfections in intermediate markets provide the opportunity for the foreign firm to build competitive advantage over its domestic counterpart (Buckley and Casson, 1976; Dunning, 1980; Hymer, 1960/1976; Rugman, 1981). The basic argument is that the firm's propensity to engage in international production depends on three necessary conditions: (1) ownership-specific (or firm-specific) advantages over incumbent domestic competitors; (2) location-specific (or country-specific) advantages that favour investment in the focal country; and (3) intermediate market failure that favours 'internalization' over other forms of contractual arrangement.

Limitations of the theory

The problem with the transaction-cost approach is that is was developed to explain how firms became international, so its utility in explaining the subsequent evolution of foreign-owned subsidiaries is not well established. As shown by Rugman and Verbeke (1992: 763), there are two assumptions in the transaction cost approach:

> First, the (sometimes implicit) assumption that an MNC's core firm-specific advantages normally originate in the parent company and that these firm-specific advantages are in principle non-location bound. Second is the assumption that country-specific advantages of host countries are mostly exogenous (e.g. a nation's factor endowments) and can only be of use in a local and static sense.

Neither of these assumptions is appropriate in large, mature MNCs so extensions to the transaction-cost theory of international production are

Table 7.1   *Summary of theoretical perspectives on the multinational firm*

	Transaction-cost theory of international production	Resource-based view of the firm	The network theory of the multinational firm
Objective function of theory	Explanation of why firms exist across national borders	Explanation of how a firm's resources can lead to competitive advantage	Description of the interrelationships between units of a firm and the system in which it is embedded
Summary of theory	International production will transpire when a firm has ownership-specific advantages over local competitors, location-specific advantages favouring local investment and intermediate market failure	A firm's resources will be a source of sustainable competitive advantage if they are (1) rare, (2) valuable, (3) hard to substitute and (4) hard to imitate	The MNC is an 'interorganizational' network of operating units, each one of which operates in its own unique local environment. The roles and activities of operating units are determined by the internal and external networks in which they are located
Implications of subsidiary initiative for the theory	The challenge is to understand how the theory can be reconciled with the phenomenon of subsidiary-driven foreign investment	The challenge is to understand how resources and capabilities developed at the subsidiary level can lead to firm-level competitive advantage	Theory is consistent with the phenomenon of subsidiary initiative. The challenge is to extend the theory in the light of this phenomenon.

necessary. These extensions are proposed by Rugman and Verbeke (ibid.) as follows:

- Firm-specific advantages can be both location-bound and non-location-bound. The former can only be exploited in a particular location, and typically lead to benefits of local responsiveness. The latter can be exploited globally and typically lead to economies of scale or scope.
- Non-location-bound advantages need not necessarily originate within the parent company, but may also be created by a subsidiary unit.
- Country-specific advantages can be used in a leveraged way (not just in a static sense) especially when contributing to the development of new firm-specific advantages.

A number of other limitations of the transaction cost approach can also be mentioned. First, Dunning's (1980) three factors (ownership, location and internalization) cannot be rigorously applied to a subsidiary-level study because they reinforce and interact with one another. When the subsidiary has interdependencies with the parent company and other subsidiaries, it is not possible to disentangle, for example, the internalization and location-advantage rationales for investment (Dunning, 1988). Moreover it should also be underlined that an investment decision is often made in large part by the subsidiary management, whereas in traditional theory it would be a home-country decision.

It is important to note that all the above modifications are designed to adapt this theory to the empirical realities of the present day. Rugman and Verbeke's (1992) objective was to reconcile the theory with Bartlett and Ghoshal's *Transnational Solution* (1989). Essentially, the task here is similar, in that one is trying to make sense of the emergence of important value-adding activities in the subsidiary through a theoretical lens that was not really designed for the task. The result is a theory that is – with some tweaking – consistent with the empirical evidence. Whether this theory then offers any additional insights into the phenomenon under investigation is more debatable.

Applying the theory to initiative-driven investment

Building on Rugman and Verbeke's (1992) modifications, let us consider how subsidiary initiative can be reconciled with the transaction cost theory of international production.

The relevant unit of analysis is an investment in the subsidiary. Using the terms already introduced, such an investment is obviously located outside the parent company and it is 'non-location-bound' meaning that it has value beyond the immediate country in which it is located.

For this investment to succeed it has to have both firm-specific and country-specific advantages. That is, there have to be certain firm-specific advantages in the subsidiary that allow the investment to overcome its 'liability of foreignness', and there have to be certain country-specific advantages to make that location, rather than any other, the optimum one for the investment.

But as discussed in Chapter 6, investments in the subsidiary are of two generic types – parent-driven investment and subsidiary-driven charter enhancement. Parent-driven investments fit neatly with the theory because they typically involve an explicit comparison of firm-specific advantages (which foreign subsidiary has the best record with this sort of manufacturing investment?) and country-specific advantages (what are the relative costs and benefits of investing in France rather than England?). Subsidiary-driven investments are less easily reconciled with the theory because they typically do not involve an explicit comparison of subsidiaries or countries. Often the subsidiary will present parent company managers with a *fait accompli*, in terms of a product or technology they have already been working on and the underlying capabilities that are necessary to succeed.

The key point is that the subsidiary's capabilities are built up in a path-dependent manner over time and as a function of the context in which they are developed. The *context* is vital here, because it refers to aspects of the local business environment that are country-specific. In other words, over time country-specific advantages become intertwined with firm-specific advantages, to the extent that they can no longer be separated. Rugman and Verbeke (1992: 763) make essentially the same point when they discuss country-specific advantages that contribute to the development of new firm-specific advantages.

The simple conclusion from this discussion, then, is that when considering investments that are driven by the subsidiary, *the two categories of firm-specific and country-specific advantages collapse into a single category of 'subsidiary-specific' advantages* (cf. Moore, 1994). The competitiveness of the subsidiary is achieved through a long-term development process, involving the transfer of resources and capabilities from the corporate system and the application of local-country learning. To attribute this competitiveness to firm- or country-specific factors would be very difficult, and probably beside the point.

No further discussion of the transaction cost theory of international production will be attempted here. It can indeed be extended to explain the phenomenon of subsidiary-driven investment but other theories appear to provide much greater insights. Entrepreneurship theory, as discussed in Chapter 5, is certainly more relevant, as is the network theory of the MNC that is discussed in the Chapter 8.

The resource-based view of the firm

The resource-based view models the firm as a bundle of heterogeneous resources and capabilities, and seeks to understand how these resources and capabilities can be a source of sustainable competitive advantage for the firm. In its simplest form, the resource-based view argues that resources that are valuable, rare and non-imitable provide the basis of competitive advantage (Barney, 1991), though it should be acknowledged that this portrayal does not begin to do justice to the enormous literature that has built up on the subject over the last decade.

Level of analysis: firm vs subsidiary

As in Chapter 5, there is a level of analysis issue that needs to be addressed upfront. The resource-based view (RBV) is a firm-level theory that is concerned with understanding how a firm (as a whole) can achieve and sustain competitive advantage. In its current form it does not give explicit attention to the subfirm level of analysis – the business unit, subsidiary or division. The firm is implicitly modelled as a monolithic entity.

This approach contrast sharply with the focus of this book, which is on the processes and activities undertaken in the subsidiary unit. The argument that has been made in previous chapters, and will be made again here, is that the subsidiary unit of an MNC is in many ways directly comparable to an autonomous firm. These subsidiaries can take initiatives to shape their own strategic direction. And they have resources and capabilities that are to some extent separable from those of their sister units around the world. The point, in other words, is that the resource-based view can be usefully applied at the level of the subsidiary. Such an approach can help us better understand the subsidiary *and* inform our thinking on the achievement of competitive advantage in the MNC as a whole.

Resources and capabilities

While there are no universally accepted definitions of the terms resources and capabilities, those proposed by Amit and Schoemaker (1993) are a good starting point. Thus *resources* are the stock of available factors owned or controlled by the firm, and *capabilities* are a firm's capacity to deploy resources, usually in combination, using organizational processes to effect a desired end.

Table 7.2 is an attempt to divide resources and capabilities into levels of analysis. 'Firm' refers to the MNC in its entirety; 'subsidiary' refers to a specific organizational unit in its geographical context. Note that the geographical location is very important, because capabilities are often 'sticky' and to some degree specific to the context in which they were developed.

If one considers resources first, most tangible resources (plant, equipment, people) are held primarily at the subsidiary level, while most intangible resources (financial, organizational, reputational) are held at

Table 7.2 *Examples of resources and capabilities at two levels of analysis*

	Subsidiary level	Firm level
Resources	• Physical resources such as plant, equipment and locally sourced raw materials • Human resources employed in the subsidiary • Reputation with local customers and suppliers	• Financial resources such as firm's borrowing capacity • Access to suppliers that is controlled centrally • Organizational resources such as the formal reporting system • Technological resources such as patents or trademarks
Capabilities	• Rapid product innovation • Lean production system • Effective distribution • Customer-focused marketing • Data processing skills	• Firm-specific capabilities such as an organizational culture supporting innovation, quality etc. • Ability to leverage capabilities from the left-hand column on a firm-wide basis

Source: Adapted from Grant, 1998

the firm level. Of course there are plenty of exceptions to this rule, such as employees or equipment that are moved between locations, or a reputation that is specific to the local subsidiary, but the key point is that it is possible to make such a split in the first place.

Capabilities are much harder to split between firm and subsidiary levels of analysis. Some are clearly held at a firm level and shared across subsidiaries, such as a particular organizational culture. Others are more likely to be specific to a particular subsidiary, such as handling local labour relations or working with government contracts. Most capabilities, however, sit somewhere between the two levels. Consider a hypothetical example such as total quality manufacturing in the Ford Motor Company. Ford probably has around 30 manufacturing plants around the world. Quality levels are measured in each plant, and it is found that year after year the highest quality ratings are achieved by the same plant in Belgium. The Belgian plant is therefore used as the benchmark that other plants should strive for, and it receives a stream of visitors from these other plants, all of whom are seeking to learn from the plant and apply its 'best practice'. Every year their quality levels creep up, but so does the quality of the Belgian plant.

So is the total quality management capability held at the level of the Belgian plant or at the firm level? The answer is a bit of both. The capability somehow originated in the Belgian plant, but it has also been successfully leveraged on a firm-wide basis. The suggestion, in other words, is that many capabilities have their origin in a single location. The extent to which such capabilities are dispersed throughout the firm depends on the ability of the firm to identify and leverage them – the so called 'transfer of best practices'. It also depends on the extent to which they are effective in different contexts – the adoption of Japanese approaches to lean production in the US, for example.

Subsidiary-level resources and capabilities

This discussion suggests that many of the firm's resources and capabilities are actually developed at the subsidiary level. Chapter 6 provided a very thorough analysis of the process of capability development in the subsidiary unit, so it does not have to be repeated here. What is necessary, however, is a more explicit discussion of the interaction between a subsidiary's capabilities and its local context. Figure 7.1 illustrates a simple model of the subsidiary in terms of its charter, capabilities and context.

As discussed in Chapter 6, a charter is the business, or elements of a business, that the subsidiary undertakes on behalf of the MNC and for which it has responsibility. A charter is essentially a licence, franchise or mandate that the firm grants to the subsidiary because it believes the subsidiary can manage the charter effectively. But such a charter is not granted in perpetuity. As the IBM Greenock case in Chapter 4 showed, charters can and do change locations, and as such they do not *define* the subsidiary. They are merely an expression of what the subsidiary is doing at any given time.

The heart of the subsidiary is its resources and capabilities. Capabilities develop over time as a function of the resource base of the subsidiary (and its local context – see below), and as a function of the activities it undertakes in the fulfilment of its charter. But while capabilities tend to be a reflection of the subsidiary's charter, they are unlikely to map exactly onto it because both are continuously evolving. Instead, capabilities evolve both in anticipation of and in reaction to changes in the subsidiary's charter.

Finally, the subsidiary's resources and capabilities are physically located in a local context, from which they draw and to which they

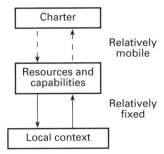

Figure 7.1   *A model of the MNC subsidiary*

contribute. In comparison with the charter-resources interface, which is relatively fluid, the resources-context interface is extremely 'sticky', though perhaps becoming less sticky over time through the globalization process. Most subsidiary units have a clear physical location that does not change, although there are a few exceptions – Pharmacia & Upjohn moving its head office from Windsor to New Jersey for example. As a general rule, physical and human resources are either too expensive or too reluctant to move, and the associated capabilities are so intertwined with the existing resources that they cannot be moved either. Moreover the capabilities of the subsidiary are often very much a function of the relationships its people have with the local milieu – formal supplier and customer relationships, and informal ties connecting individual employees to the local social network. In short the argument is simply that geographical location matters – as the soil in which the subsidiary's root system is established and as the stimulus for the development of specific capabilities.

This discussion helps clarify an important point, namely that the criteria used to evaluate resources in the RBV (valuable, rare, non-imitable, non-substitutable) are not really relevant at the subsidiary level. Because the subsidiary is just one part of the whole, its resources and capabilities need to be complementary to other resources and capabilities elsewhere in the corporation, not necessarily unique. Each building block has a value in itself, but it is the ability to put those blocks together in a unique, non-imitable way that is the source of advantage, not the individual value of the various blocks. As seen in cases of acquisition, the price the buyer is prepared to pay is not a function of the stand-alone value of the acquired firm's resources, but of how much those resources are worth when combined with the buying firm's resources.

So returning to the terms used in the last section, the subsidiary's resources and capabilities have to be non-location-bound (meaning they can be leveraged in multiple locations) and they have to be superior to those available elsewhere in the corporation to meet the criteria of firm-specific and/or country-specific advantage. But they do not have to be unique or hard to imitate *per se* because those criteria apply only at the firm level.

Firm-level resources and capabilities

This discussion will help clarify the role of the firm-level management in building competitive advantage through its resources. There are two elements. First, they have to gain access to and/or develop resources and capabilities that can be applied across the entire firm. This includes such things as developing a corporate culture that supports innovation, managing the firm's intellectual property and so on. Second, they have to put in place systems to leverage subsidiary-level capabilities on a firm-wide basis. The challenge, in such systems, is to find a way of taking the capabilities out of the context in which they were developed and applying them to other contextual settings. This is by no means impossible – witness the great success of Japanese transplant factories in the automobile industry – but it does require a great sensitivity to the problems that can arise in the transfer of capabilities. As a means of illustrating the complexity of this process, the following are some of the more popular systems that firms use to facilitate the transfer of capabilities between locations:

- *Knowledge management systems*, for keeping track of valuable capabilities used in one place that could be applied elsewhere.
- *Centres of excellence*, which are 'best practices' recognized by the corporation with a view to the practice being made available to other units in the corporation.
- *'Model plants'*, which are replicated in their entirety in new locations around the world when expansion is needed.
- *'League tables'*, which chart the performance of R&D centres, manufacturing plants or marketing units in key areas such as productivity, quality or market share. These tables are designed to highlight the differences in practices between units, and therefore to encourage the weaker performers to learn from the higher performers.
- *Personnel management systems*, such as secondments, transfers and international training programmes. Such approaches aid in the informal transfer of capabilities between units.

The link to competitive advantage

To take this discussion back to the basic premises of the resource-based view of the firm, it should be apparent that *competitive advantage based on resources is built at the corporate level*. If the subsidiary units are the building blocks, the ability to put the building blocks together is held at the corporate level, and it is *that* capability that is the source of competitive advantage. If one consider Ericsson's R&D activities, for example, which occur in more than 40 units around the world, it is widely recognized that the ability to undertake decentralized development is one of the key capabilities of the firm. If any one unit was sold, Ericsson's R&D capacity would remain more or less undiminished.

This observation leads us to the role of the corporate centre. In the Ericsson case, the implication is that there is a rather sophisticated corporate-level capability for managing the firm's dispersed development capability. In more general terms, it suggests there needs to be some sort of overarching capability at the corporate level that facilitates the coordination of individual units in unique ways – a sort of 'network management capability'.

But there is an interesting dilemma when one pursues this line of thinking. In Chapters 5 and 8 the argument is that the firm is best seen as an internal market, in which individual units compete with one another and the corporate centre plays a minimal role. Here, in contrast, the argument is that competitive advantage accrues to firms that have the capability to combine and coordinate the dispersed activities of its subsidiary units. This in turn implies that there have to be overarching capabilities at the corporate level to make such coordination possible.

The fact is that these two different conclusions are hard to reconcile. This is true in terms of both theory and practice. All successful organizational forms are, it seems, built on such internal tensions. To go back to Lawrence and Lorsch (1967) for example, there is a continuous trade-off between differentiation and integration. Here the trade-off is building internal competition to ensure that every unit acts like an autonomous firm, and between building corporate-level capabilities that ensure that individual units can be put together in unique, value-added ways. Thus it is always possible to enlarge the list of roles that the corporate centre plays, but the point is that the more one enlarges it, the more one takes away from the purity of the internal market system.

The network theory of the MNC

Attempts to model the MNC as some form of interorganizational network have been going on for about 10 years, but the idea that network thinking can be used *within* the MNC has existed for much longer (for example Emerson, 1962). Moreover, as pointed out by Ghoshal and Bartlett (1990), the MNC is a particularly interesting case for examining interorganizational relationships because it exists in a differentiated task environment, in which each unit has both its internal network relationships (to sister units and to HQ) and its external network relationships (to the local marketplace and beyond). This network perspective has become very influential in recent literature on the MNC, and indeed has been an important foundation for the current work.

Three characteristics of the network model are particularly relevant to the study of subsidiary initiative. First, every unit (the subsidiary in this case) is a semi-autonomous entity that has considerable discretion to decide the nature and frequency of its exchange relationships with other actors. This 'loose coupling' with the rest of the corporation is crucial to the idea of initiative, because it indicates that the head office does not have the power to prevent entrepreneurial endeavours, even if wants to. The second key characteristic of the network model is that the subsidiary has both internal and external relationships. When one thinks in terms of initiative, then, the subsidiary can be alert to opportunities in both its internal and its external network. And as argued in Chapter 5, the two different networks have very different implications for the development of the MNC. Finally, it was observed in Chapter 5 that the MNC can be usefully modelled as an internal market. The implications of this were examined with regard to the Schumpeterian and Kirznerian forms of entrepreneurship, but there is enormous scope for playing out other implications, such as the role of internal competition between subsidiary units as a driver of firm competitiveness.

In sum, the network theory of the MNC is wholly consistent with the ideas presented in this book, but it simply does not go far enough. Opportunities for extending or refining this theory have been hinted at throughout the book, so it is appropriate now to give these thoughts a more systematic treatment. This will be the subject of Chapter 8.

Key ideas in Chapter 7

- There are three relevant theories of the MNC: (1) the transaction cost economics approach; (2) the network approach; and (3) the resource-based view of the firm. This chapter has discussed the first and last of these in detail, reserving discussion of the network approach to Chapter 8.
- Transaction cost economics argues that MNCs exist as mechanisms for internalizing transactions in which market failure occurs. However, while transaction cost economics is valuable as a way of explaining how firms become international in the first place, it is less relevant for understanding how established international firms function on a global basis. Subsidiary initiative is difficult but not impossible to reconcile with transaction cost economics. A key point is to recognize that firm-specific advantages and country-specific advantages can not be separated in the case of subsidiary initiative. Instead the concept of subsidiary-specific advantages needs to be introduced.
- The resource-based view of the firm models the MNC as a bundle of heterogeneous resources and capabilities. The main problem here is the appropriate level of analysis. Traditionally the theory has viewed the firm as a monolithic entity. The focus in this book on the subsidiary shows clearly that many – though not all – resources and capabilities are held at the subsidiary level. For those resources and capabilities, it is important for the MNC that processes are put in place to tap into, transfer and leverage them on a corporate-wide basis. Competitive advantage is built up not so much through the possession of unique or hard-to-imitate resources, as by being able to combine and integrate subsidiary-level resources in novel ways.

8

An Internal Market Perspective on the Multinational Corporation

This is the final theoretical chapter of the book (Chapter 9 discusses the managerial implications of the research) and as such it serves two functions. First, it pulls together many of the concepts and issues discussed in earlier chapters. Second, it represents a departure point for a new way of thinking about the nature of the MNC, based on the idea of the MNC as an *internal market*. This internal market model differs only by degree from related models such as the heterarchy or the transnational model, but the differences are more than just semantic and they offer some interesting avenues for further enquiry.

In the first section some of the major issues that MNCs are facing will be summarized. There is some repetition here, but the idea is to present a logical and internally consistent argument rather than just presenting the internal market model as a *fait accompli*. After that the elements of the new model will be presented.

Issues facing large MNCs

MNCs are facing a number of important changes that fall broadly under the 'globalization' banner. As stated at the outset, this book is more about internally driven change than adaptation to a changing world, but it is worth at least mentioning those drivers of globalization that are an important element of the process of change under investigation here:

- *Economic change*, specifically increasing free trade within and between trading blocs, increasing mobility of capital and increasing openness to inward investment.
- *Technological change*, especially the rapidly increasing ability to co-ordinate international activities such as product development through electronic media.
- *Global competition*, driven by the growth ambitions of firms in both developed and developing nations, and the never-ending search for economies of scale and scope.

Taken together, and in combination with the internally driven processes described in Chapters 2 to 4, we are witnessing major changes in the strategies and structures of MNCs. Three types of change appear to be particularly important.

First, *there has been a de facto increase in the geographical dispersal of value-adding activities in most large MNCs.* The term *de facto* is used to indicate that such dispersal is not always planned. There is a strong 'push' component driven by the efforts of MNC managers to build up a presence in major overseas markets, counter the threats presented by competitors and gain access to leading-edge ideas or low-cost factors of production. There is also a strong 'pull' component that is driven by the efforts of host-country governments to bring in additional inward investment, and by the initiative of subsidiary managers who are attempting to develop their own operations. Finally, some geographical dispersal is an unintended consequence of other strategic actions, such as international acquisitions or strategic alliances. The net result of these factors is that – by accident *and* design – most large firms are undertaking larger amounts of their value-adding activity outside the home country, which is making the job of managing large MNCs much harder.

Second, *competitive pressures are pushing MNCs to make better use of their geographically dispersed activities* – to make them more efficient and to coordinate them more effectively. Nowhere is this clearer than in formerly polycentric firms such as Philips, Electrolux, Johnson & Johnson and Shell, all of which have come to understand that they can no longer justify the cost of stand-alone country operations. These firms have all rationalized their manufacturing and R&D activities, but typically by assigning 'world mandates' to subsidiary companies rather than by recentralizing them in the home country. A related trend is the emergence of 'centres of excellence' in subsidiary companies, which are typically pockets of expertise that the firm wants to disseminate to other operations around the world.

A key driver of these changes is benchmarking, which enables firms to quantify their relative efficiency in any given process or activity. Its ubiquitous use is having a major impact on the configuration and coordination of firms' global operations. *Internal* benchmarking allows firms to compare related operations in different locations, resulting in performance league tables, best practice transfers and the emergence of centres of excellence. It also stimulates internal competition between operations for future investment. *External* benchmarking helps firms to identify which of their activities or practices are substandard, which in turn drives performance improvement programmes, decisions to relocate to lower-cost locations or decisions to outsource activities to specialized suppliers. Again, this change is a gradual one that has been going on for decades, but its net effect is further to emphasize the relative locational advantages of certain countries (low-cost labour, tax breaks, the presence of key competitors and so on) and to push geographical dispersal yet further.

Third, *MNCs are recognizing the need to develop more flexible configurations to make them more responsive to changing market demands.*

This issue is somewhat more sector-specific than the first two, but in industries as different as automobiles, telecommunications, pharmaceuticals and insurance, managers have been heard to emphasize the need to become better at developing new technologies, identifying emerging market needs, cannibalizing existing products and so on. Of course this is not a new issue, and neither is it unique to MNCs, but it is mentioned here because the *response* that many MNCs are experimenting with is to push their foreign subsidiaries to be far more entrepreneurial, and this obviously is a multinational-specific issue.

Elements of a new model

So what is the implication of these changes for the MNC? Throughout this book 'elements' of an emerging model have been identified. These elements are typically based on cases that the author has observed first-hand. They are summarized in the following paragraphs.

The first point to make is that *the discussion of strategy, organization and competitive advantage needs to be framed at a lower level of analysis*. The subsidiary unit is the chosen level in this book, but it may be just as appropriate to look at the value-adding activity or process. There are several reasons for this:

- Benchmarking leads to an evaluation of competitiveness at the level of the activity or process, because that is the level where comparison can accurately be made. Once this has been done, all subsequent related action – transfer of best practice, identification of centre of excellence, outsourcing – must also take place at the activity or process level.
- Greater geographical dispersal makes it very hard to pretend that the MNC is a monolithic entity. Each subsidiary unit, by virtue of its geographical location, has a unique set of network relationships, and to some extent also has its own unique history. Even if that subsidiary is bundled organizationally with other units in different countries, it is likely to retain a unique identity.
- As argued in Chapter 7, capabilities are in large part built at the unit level. Of course capabilities can exist at multiple levels in the corporation, and some are corporate-wide. But the proven value of benchmarking attests to the existence of important capabilities that emerge in certain locations. And research into knowledge management (Szulanski, 1996; Zander, 1991) shows how hard it can be to transfer effectively such capabilities to other locations.
- The demand for greater efficiency is pushing consolidation at the activity level. On the R&D side, rather than create a single worldwide R&D operation, firms are more likely to end up with three or four

operations, each with a specific technology mandate. In the manu-facturing sector, firms are moving to focused factories that have global responsibility for a single product line or family of products. Dedi-cated distribution or logistics centres are being created. Treasury management, call centres, HR training and a host of other support activities are being pulled out of the existing infrastructure, and set up as stand-alone, Europe-wide operations.

The important point is that progress in understanding the strategy and organization of the MNC cannot easily be made by treating it as a monolithic entity. As Hedlund (1994) points out, the M-form organization works on the basis of division, which creates order and efficiency but drives out creativity and flexibility. Instead he advocates an N-form based on novelty and recombination. The point here is essentially the same – competitive advantage is ultimately built up at the corporate level, but it is achieved through the effective bringing together of capabilities and market relationships built up at the subsidiary level.

The second point is that there is *increasing internal competition between subsidiary units* (and indeed between other entities such as product divisions, R&D centres and factories). The cases described in Chapters 2 and 3, for example, hinted at the process of internal competition. On more detailed inspection, two major types of internal competition can be identified:

- Internal competition for a charter, or the responsibility to perform certain activities for the corporation as a whole. For example Volks-wagen recently awarded the global charter for the New Beetle produc-tion to its Mexican subsidiary, after considering competing bids from other plants around the world.
- Internal competition for a customer (in the next stage of the value chain). This involves two units undertaking parallel development or production work, with the decision about which is preferred only being taken once that stage is completed. Tracy Kidder's *The Soul of a New Machine* (1971), for example, documents the internal competi-tion between development groups in Data General. Such competition seems enormously wasteful because of the duplication of effort, but it can be valuable if speed to market is crucial. Thus Hewlett-Packard reputedly encourages its product divisions actively to cannibalize one another's products, rather than wait for a competitor to do it.

What is the logic behind internal competition? In part it is about making the MNC's activity base efficient, which as basic economic theory tells us is stimulated through competition. But it is also about allowing multiple options to coexist in the face of massive technological or environmental change. As noted above, the practice in Hewlett-Packard and some other MNCs is to allow divisions to take their own decisions on what technolo-gies or products the marketplace needs, so that even if one division gets it wrong, another may get it right. This approach involves some duplication, but that may be a small price to pay for not missing the next wave of technology.

The third point to make is that *charters are being actively sought by existing and new locations around the world.* Again, the underlying concepts here are well established – countries differ in their attractiveness for undertaking certain value-adding activities; industry clusters make agglomeration economies and learning opportunities available to investing firms; and certain markets have strategic significance to MNCs participating in global competition (Hamel and Prahalad, 1985; Kogut, 1985; Porter, 1990; Vernon, 1979). All these factors would predict greater dispersal of the MNC's activities around the world, and indeed all have had a considerable impact in recent decades. But the interesting shift is the shift from HQ-led *push* to host-country-led *pull.* Two factors are at work:

● Host-country economies, and cities or regions within countries, are becoming very aggressive in their pursuit of inward investment. For example there are around 55 separate investment promotion agencies in Tokyo, each one trying to persuade Japanese MNCs to invest in their country or region. Moreover these agencies are not simply providing information about their region – they are actively looking for ways to differentiate their 'offering' from that of their competitors by focusing on certain industry segments, seeking only certain types of investment and offering whatever hard and soft incentives they are allowed to. What is emerging as a result is even greater regional specialization than economic models might predict. If you want to build a European headquarters, go to Belgium; a semiconductor plant, consider Scotland and Ireland; a pharmaceutical R&D investment, New Jersey; and so on. Such investments are easy to promote by inward-investment agencies because that is where their comparative advantage lies, and they are easy to justify for the MNC.
● Subsidiary managers are increasingly seeking out incremental investments from their parent companies to build on their existing capabilities. This concept was discussed in Chapter 6 in terms of the development trajectory seen in many foreign subsidiaries, and the important role of subsidiary initiative as a driver of the process. What is particularly relevant here is that such efforts by the managers of subsidiaries are driven in large part by the pressures of outsourcing and benchmarking.

The net effect of these two factors is increasing specialization in value-adding activities according to the relative strengths and weaknesses of different regions and subsidiary units around the world. Obviously there are other factors at play and strong inertial forces that limit the speed of change, but the overall impression one gets is that the impact of differential comparative advantage and industrial clusters on the spatial configuration of MNCs is increasing.

The fourth element of the new model, which builds on the previous three, is that the *subsidiary unit needs to be understood as a set of resources and capabilities embedded in a local context, with a potentially contestable charter.* The interface between the subsidiary's charter and its resources/capabilities is semi-fluid in that charters can and do change; but the interface between the resources/capabilities of the subsidiary and its local context is very sticky. This conceptualization was described in Chapter 7.

The internal market model

In considering the changes underway in many MNCs, it seems that a combination of changes in the business environment and experimentation inside these firms is resulting in a shift towards an internal market model,[1] whereby activities are configured and coordinated through a give-and-take process of mutual adjustment between units, rather than being centrally planned and dictated by headquarters.

Before examining the specifics of the internal market model it is important to be clear that it applies only to a subset of the population of MNCs. To generalize enormously, we can see three archetypal organizational forms among large firms: the 'traditional' manufacturing firm, such as GM, which coordinates both its own operations and its suppliers on a central basis; the 'virtual' firm, such as Nike or Dell, which outsources large parts of its business system; and the 'internal market' firm, such as ABB, which continues to own most of its business system but coordinates it through a more bottom-up process (cf. Snow et al., 1992). The expectation here is that the traditional model still works reasonably well in global industries with high economies of scale, but that it is gradually being eclipsed by the virtual and the internal market models, both of which are better suited to the dynamic business environment that prevails today. The choice between the virtual and the internal market model, however, is not simple. In some respects they are quite similar, because both involve the use of market systems to facilitate coordination; but they differ in one important respect, namely that the virtual model involves the coordination of multiple independent firms whereas the internal model involves coordination within a single legal entity. While it would be interesting to compare these two models in greater detail, this chapter is explicitly concerned with the internal market model, so let us examine it in more detail.

The internal market concept is reasonably well established in the academic literature, dating back at least to March and Simon (1958). Halal et al. (1993) provide the most comprehensive overview of the concept, but it should be noted that many of the ideas behind the internal market model can also be found in other frameworks – notably the inter-organizational network of Ghoshal and Bartlett (1990), the business networks perspective (Forsgren and Johanson, 1992), Hedlund's (1986) heterarchy, and indeed the literatures on empowerment, corporate entre-preneurship, intraorganization ecology and self-organizing systems. However, far from just being another label for the same phenomenon, the internal market approach appears to reflect some of the actual changes that are underway in large MNCs at the moment, and as such it offers an important new perspective on their emerging strategies and structures.

Before getting to the key question of a 'market for what?' a few of the basic principles of the internal market approach need to be laid out.

- Internal markets allow individual units to make choices about what activities to undertake, the source of their inputs and the destination of their outputs, through the availability of alternative suppliers and customers.
- Every internal market is embedded in an external market (that is, the market economy), from which it draws and to which it contributes. The 'porosity' of this boundary is crucial, because one of the key choices a unit can make is whether to sell to or source from external units.
- Markets work in large part because of the existence of high-powered incentives (Williamson, 1991). Thus for the internal market model to work well the top management has to give extraordinary attention to the incentive system – both the 'hard' and the 'soft' components.
- The responsibility of subsidiary managers in the internal market is to maximize the performance of the subsidiary, according to the defined incentives.
- Internal markets are very good at enhancing efficiency, but not so good at enhancing effectiveness. Efficiency thus becomes the respon-sibility of subsidiary managers who are responding to the market incentives. And effectiveness becomes the responsibility of the top management, who define the appropriate incentive system and the rules of the game (see below).
- The internal market system is a theoretical lens not a normative model. Thus the approach is relevant even for MNCs that still prefer a centrally planned structure. It may indeed be in the top management's interest to *restrict* the internal market in certain cases, and certainly there is plenty of evidence of subsidiaries that rarely if ever experi-ence the workings of the internal market.

It should also be noted at this point that the internal market model under discussion here assumes that the value-adding unit is the relevant level of analysis. One could easily take the ideas down to the level of the individual – by looking at the internal labour market, how specific projects compete for key individuals and so on – but for the sake of clarity the focus here is on the unit and organization levels.

Types of internal market

While the idea of internal markets has been around for some time, the key insight here is that *subsidiary units in the MNC are participating simultaneously in at least three different internal markets*. The three discussed here are the markets for intermediate products/services, charters, and practices (Table 8.1). Other markets could probably be identified as well – a market for reputation, for services, for credibility – but for the moment they are less well established. The argument is that to understand how the large MNC really works all these internal market systems have to be considered together. Only then can we make sense of concepts such as 'subsidiary strategy' and 'corporate strategy'. Let us consider each in turn.

The market for intermediate products and services

This is the form of internal market that is the focus of Halal et al.'s (1993) book. In traditional MNCs the value-adding system is broken down into steps, and the unit responsible for each step supplies its intermediate product to the next unit in the chain. Using an internal market approach this chain is composed of discrete value-adding units, and for each unit one asks: how great a degree of choice should this unit have with regard to suppliers/customers, either inside or outside the firm? Using a traditional vertically integrated model there would be no choice at any stage, and transfer prices would essentially be mandated from above or calculated on a cost-plus basis (Eccles, 1985). Under an internal market model there might be two or more internal suppliers or customers, and there might be several external suppliers or customers as well. ABB, for example, has moved to an internal-market approach in which each business unit has more or less complete freedom about who it sells to and who it buys from. Obviously in such a system the internal transfer price has to be the same or close to the external market price.

The extent to which an internal market for intermediate products and services is created is very much a strategic issue that the top management must decide upon. There are two separate questions. First, should external customers and suppliers be used in competition with internal ones? As a general rule, such external relationships are valuable as a means of enhancing efficiency, but there are times when they can be contrary to strategic interests, for example when a new component ends up being sold into competing products. The second question is should the MNC itself maintain two or more value-adding activities acting in parallel? The costs of such duplication are of course high, but they can be beneficial, both as a means of enhancing time to market and as a means of trying out different approaches.

Of the three internal markets, this one has least specific relevance to the MNC because it is concerned with the value-adding activity, not the physical unit. Thus the discussion above gives no explicit attention to where the activity is located, it is just concerned with the extent to which multiple paths will be followed. Having said that, this form of internal market is still of vital concern to large MNCs because the size and dispersal of units around the world makes the opportunity for multiple

Table 8.1 *Types of internal market and their characteristics*

	Type 1	Type 2	Type 3
Market for:	Intermediate product or service	Charter	Capability or practice
Competition between:	Value-adding activities (regardless of where performed)	Value-adding units (the physical entities)	Value-adding units (the physical entities)
Customer:	Next stage in value chain	Resource allocator, HQ or divisional decision maker	Other value-adding units
Main question in the establishment of this market:	To what extent does the MNC want to internalize the existing market system?	Where (physically) do we want each specific value-adding activity to take place?	How can leading-edge capabilities or practices be efficiently identified and transferred?
Role of subsidiary unit:	Compete with internal and external competitors in delivery of product or service to customer	Compete with internal and external competitors for new and existing charters	Actively seek out 'suppliers' of practices, and make practices available to other units
Role of HQ:	Define extent to which each stage of value chain will be internalized, and customer's freedom to select among competing alternatives	Define extent to which new and existing charters will be competed for, and extent to which external bids will be accepted	Define systems that help to maximize flow of practices inward and internally, but which limit the outward flow of practices (to external entities)

internal sources and customers much greater. ABB, again, is a classic example of this.

The market for charters

The internal market for charters is most visible in cases of new investments – a new production plant, an R&D centre or a logistics centre. In such cases, as indicated earlier, there are likely to be multiple subsidiary units and inward investment bodies clamouring for the opportunity to receive that investment. Here the strategic decision by the top management is twofold: defining the criteria by which the investment decision will be made, and, more relevant to this discussion, deciding how open to make the competition for the charter. On this issue, MNCs today run the full spectrum, ranging from no choice at all ('we need to make a strategic investment in China'), to the identification of a small number of candidate locations that are then evaluated, to very open competition that is broadcast to all subsidiary units around the world. Again, external competitors are often considered, depending on how strategic the investment in question is.

While new investments are almost always actively competed for, it was argued earlier that *existing* charters are increasingly deemed to be mobile and therefore open to competition. This may be the most interesting element of the internal market model, because it represents a much more fundamental shift in how activities within the MNC are allocated. New investments have always been competed for, but the idea that a subsidiary could lose a charter for failing to perform, just as weak companies go bankrupt in the open market, is a relatively new one to most MNCs.

What are the costs and benefits of internal market competition for charters? The benefits are – as above – increased efficiency in operations and an increased level of self-sufficiency on the part of subsidiary units. The costs are of two types. First, making this form of market work is quite expensive because proposals have to be evaluated. Unlike the first type of internal market, which operates through a form of invisible hand, charter decisions have to be judged by the top management or some form of review board. The second cost is analogous to structural employment in the market system. If a unit loses its charter, its employees are essentially out of work, and it is therefore in the MNC's interests to find a way of relocating them, to find them a new charter or perhaps even to outplace them. All of which are costly options.

The internal market for charters is central to the working of the modern MNC. As the subsidiary model developed in Chapter 6 indicated, charters are mobile and competed-for, while the subsidiary's resources, capabilities and local context are the differentiating factors by which it competes for charters. Subsidiary strategy, as the next section will explain, is therefore about building a sustainable position *vis-à-vis* both internal and external competitors.

The market for capabilities and practices

The third type of internal market is for capabilities and practices, and it is most visible in cases of best-practice transfer between sites (see, for example, Arvidsson, 1999; Szulanski, 1996; Zander, 1991). But this market differs in one important respect from the other two, namely that the competitive element is missing. 'Buying' units are those in search of a new practice, and they can potentially access that practice from any other internal unit as well as from countless external operations. But of course the 'selling' unit, the one transferring its best practice, typically does not receive any material reward for that service, and as a result the market for practices does not work at all efficiently. The challenge, with which many MNCs are experimenting, is to provide the appropriate incentives to encourage best-practice transfers between units. These can include structural approaches such as the creation of centres of excellence and softer approaches such as evaluating individuals' propensity to cooperate with individuals in other units.[2] A complementary approach, which can be seen in some firms, is the emergence of 'brokers' in the market for practices, whose specific role is to link up buyers and sellers.

The internal market for practices, then, is rather different from the other two but is no less important because it helps to make all units more efficient. Internal benchmarking, as noted earlier, is one manifestation of a more active internal market for best practices, and the interest among scholars in knowledge transfers is also testament to the growing importance of this phenomenon.

Two more points are also very relevant to the discussion of internal markets for practices. First, the efficiency of the internal market is important as a means of ensuring that best practices are spread around, but perhaps even more important are the links with the external market in which the MNC is embedded. External benchmarking studies, imitation of competitors, diffusion of practices from customers, links to consulting companies and so on are all mechanisms for facilitating the inward flow of practices into the internal market. But while inward flows are essential, it is equally important for the MNC that outward flows are *restricted*, lest proprietary practices are given away to competitors. The internal market for practices, in other words, ideally should be designed so that it is permeable in one direction only.

The second point is that while the first two forms of internal markets require sister units to compete with one another – for margins or charters – the market for practices requires them to cooperate and to share freely with one another. Interestingly the schizophrenia that requires units to cooperate and compete at the same time seems to work quite well in practice. HP and Ericsson, for example, both seem to do a good job of managing the balance, perhaps because of the strong corporate culture in both cases, and perhaps because their incentive systems are well designed to reward both behaviours.

Conclusions

The internal market model suggests a number of different implications for both theory and practice. One key insight is that two distinct levels of strategy emerge. The lower level is the subsidiary unit, or perhaps the factory, the R&D centre or the division. Such units become semi-autonomous entities *responsible for their own destiny*. They remain as members of the internal market in which practices are shared and various corporate assets such as technology are commonly owned, but they also actively compete with various internal and external units. Viewed in this way, the concept of a subsidiary 'strategy' becomes much more real. Subsidiary initiative can be seen as simply the action of a responsible subsidiary manager who is looking for ways of enhancing the competitiveness of his or her operation. And certain strategic actions, such as developing a unique technology or being the highest-quality plant in the MNC, begin to make sense as analogues to Porter's (1980) generic strategies.

The higher level of strategy is the corporate level. In terms of the internal market model, the corporate management's job is to define the rules of the game – how much internal competition will be allowed, the criteria for awarding charters, defining appropriate incentive systems to make the markets function and so on. But as noted earlier, internal markets are primarily designed to enhance efficiency, so an equally or more important part of the corporate management's role is to steer the MNC's effectiveness. This means, amongst other things, defining which markets and technologies to enter, defining the MNC's competitive positioning and creating the ability to adapt to changing environmental conditions. All of these can *to some degree* be achieved through the definition of the internal markets – for example, by allowing internal competition in the consumer marketplace the MNC becomes flexible to changes in customer tastes; and by tilting the criteria for awarding charters towards quality and service measures, the MNC defines its overall competitive positioning. But eventually there will be occasions when the corporate management has to step in and overrule the resource allocations made by the internal market. As argued by Moran and Ghoshal (1999), firms are not just a second-best solution to markets in the case of market failure. They are substantially different, primarily in terms of their ability to create value. So the internal market metaphor is useful, but only if the corporate management recognizes that it also has its limits.

The question of multinationality

This brings us back full-circle to the issue with which this book began. It was argued that many of the changes we see taking place are a function of internally driven change in the MNC. In this chapter the elements of a new model of the MNC have been sketched out, based on the idea of internal markets. In doing this it has taken a 'bottom-up' perspective that started with the subsidiary unit *in its local context* as the basic building block. The MNC, in other words, can be modelled as a federation or a network of interdependent subsidiary units, whose geographical location matters because it is the link to the local context and the development of location-specific capabilities, which provide the basis for the subsidiaries' competitiveness.

An important point in this argument is that the question of multi-nationality *per se* is still vitally important. Indeed the process of globalization is making it even more important because the geographical dispersal of firms' value-adding activities continues to increase. It is also quite appealing to bring the idea of internal markets into the management literature. The well-established theory explaining why MNCs exist is of course built on the idea that MNCs' internalize the market for intermediate products. Here, the idea of an internal market is being broadened to include not just the market for intermediate products but also the market for charters and practices.

Key ideas in Chapter 8

- The MNC is described using the metaphor of the internal market. This is a way of arguing, as others have done, that the MNC is a set of interconnected but semi-autonomous subsidiary operations that are embedded in a broader set of relationships with other actors. The new development here is that the subsidiary is seen as participating in a number of internal markets – a market for products and components, a market for charters (that is, the franchise to make or sell something for the MNC) and a market for practices. These markets shape the resource allocation process inside the MNC.
- Central to the internal market is the idea that subsidiaries *compete* with one another – for new charters, for investment funds, for management talent. Internal competition of this kind should be encouraged as long as it does not reduce managers' ability to cooperate with each other, or result in excessive levels of duplication.
- The subsidiary manager's role in the internal market system is to define the *strategy* of the subsidiary as if it were a discrete entity.
- The corporate manager's role in the internal market system is about defining the rules of the game in which subsidiary managers compete. It is also about being prepared to step in from time to time and overrule decisions that would have been optimum from a market perspective, but would have deleterious consequences for the MNC as a whole.

Notes

1   Some readers will not find the internal market terminology to their liking. Firms, it is argued, are very different from markets, and should be understood on the basis of their considerable talent for value creation rather than as failed markets. This point is accepted. Nonetheless, it is argued that the internal market metaphor is a useful analytical device for revealing some of the unique ways in which firms are able to create value, as well as some of the chief limitations of firms. The reality is that firms use a variety of firm-like and market-like systems all the time, so our academic models may as well reflect the empirical phenomenon under investigation.

2   Interestingly, though, it is hard to find any firms that use monetary incentives. Presumably the concern with such a system is that the true value of practices is hard to measure, so all sorts of suboptimal behaviours would emerge, such as less-capable units trying to sell their practices to others in the hope of reward.

9

Implications for Management Practice

It is interesting to note that there appear to be no applied books written for the benefit of the subsidiary manager. Several well-known volumes (for example, Bartlett and Ghoshal, 1989; Prahalad and Doz, 1987) have been written to guide the top management of large MNCs in their strategy formulation and implementation, but the subsidiary-level counterpart does not exist. One possible reason for this is that the target audience is too small, but it seems likely that there is another, more delicate factor at work as well, namely that the sort of advice that subsidiary managers need to hear is somewhat heretical when viewed from the parent-company manager's perspective. And such advice is often best left unstated, because it draws its value from its ambiguity. When asked why they have sponsored a local investment, for example, subsidiary managers will always express their arguments in terms of the strength of the local economy, the capabilities of the subsidiary, or the strategic importance of the country, all of which are the sorts of rationale that head office managers would use themselves. But deep down one can be fairly confident that the managers in question are also acting to varying degrees in the interests of their employees, their own country (if they are local employees) and their own self-gratification. There is nothing wrong with that, of course, if such actions stimulate higher levels of passion and involvement in the subsidiary's employees; and it is often possible to reconcile such selfish motives with the greater good of the corporation. But the point is that such arguments are not the sort of things head office managers want to hear, so they go unstated.

The purpose of this chapter is to pick up on some of these rather delicate issues and to play out their implications for subsidiary and head office managers. This chapter will, however, stop short of offering specific advice to either group, primarily because this *is* an academic book. Perhaps the much-needed book of advice to subsidiary managers will follow, but for the moment any manager who happens to pick up this book will have to accept these managerial 'implications' as being the closest thing they will find to prescriptive advice.

This chapter is divided into four sections. The first two deal with the perspective of the subsidiary manager and the head office manager, respectively, by looking at the sorts of action they should take if they are to manage subsidiary initiative and subsidiary evolution effectively. The third section looks at how subsidiary initiative affects the dynamics of the parent–subsidiary relationship over time. The final section examines, from a managerial perspective, some of the concerns that are frequently raised about subsidiary initiative.

Thoughts for the subsidiary manager

As should be abundantly clear by now, this book is suggesting a rather more entrepreneurial approach to subsidiary management than that which is traditionally found in large MNCs. This entrepreneurial approach is manifested at two levels: at the level of the individual initiative and at the level of the subsidiary's long-term strategy. Let us take each in turn.

Managing the initiative

Specific initiatives are typically directed towards a process of charter change in the subsidiary, such as winning a new manufacturing investment, gaining responsibility for an export market or achieving a centre of excellence. As shown in Chapter 3, initiatives take two basic forms, internal and external, which require very different strategies to be successful.

Internal initiatives are directed towards opportunities within the internal market system – either planned corporate investments for which the subsidiary bids, or attempts to reconfigure the existing internal arrangements. As shown in Chapters 2 and 3, some subsidiary managers are very conscious of their own unit's strengths and weaknesses, and are frequently on the lookout for new activities to dovetail with their present capabilities. The case of IBM in Greenock, Scotland, for example, involved the subsidiary first of all colocating a monitor development group that had been based in London, and then identifying the order-fulfilment and help-centre functions as Europe-wide activities that could be centralized in Greenock.

In terms of key success factors, internal initiatives rely on two things. First, and in marked contrast to external initiatives, internal initiatives need a relatively high degree of integration into the corporate system. Subsidiary managers involved in such initiatives emphasize that it is important for them to be tied into the corporate network so that they became aware of investment opportunities at the earliest possible time. As one manager observed, 'the best way to win a competitive investment is to write the specifications'. One 3M Canada manager, for example, accidentally heard about an embryonic investment plan on a routine visit to St Paul, Minnesota, which subsequently led to a $20 million investment in Canada.

Second, the subsidiary has to have, or be prepared to work hard for, a reputation as a trustworthy and reliable operation. Subsidiary managers are typically confronted with a simple implicit challenge: why would we risk investing in a foreign country when we can stick with tried and tested solutions closer to home? The response is often to mitigate the risk by capitalizing on personal contacts at HQ. In other cases, such as IBM Scotland, initiative success is built on the back of many years of manufacturing excellence. In the absence of either contacts or reputation, however, the subsidiary's prospects are rather limited.

Because they involve a significant level of risk for HQ managers, internal initiatives are pursued through a rather orthodox line of attack through the formal lines of authority. Monsanto Canada's dry glyphosate initiative, as described in Chapter 2, led to the establishment of a group whose role was to assess four possible locations for the new agrochemical investment. Similarly 3M Canada (Chapter 4) pursued several initiatives aimed at winning new manufacturing investments in Canada, each of which had to pass through two operating committees in the US. The process was methodical and incremental, with subsidiary management gradually moving up through the corporate hierarchy, building support and commitment from all the key individuals. Often this process took up to a year. In one case the initiative was put on hold for two years until the arrival of a new manufacturing director in the US who was more amenable to the proposal.

Two additional tactics can be observed in internal initiatives. One is a two-pronged approach. The initiative champion makes a formal proposal through the official lines of authority. At the same time the subsidiary president utilizes his personal contacts at a much higher level in the HQ to build legitimacy for the proposal and smooth its course through the system. The second is the use of a *quid pro quo*, some sort of concession by the subsidiary to compensate the losing party. For example the Honeywell Canada proposal, mentioned in Chapter 2, encountered strong resistance from the plant in Minnesota that was making the products for the US. However a deal was negotiated whereby the Toronto plant would swap its other manufacturing responsibilities for the exclusive production of zone valves and fan and limit devices. Both plants ended up shedding a few jobs, but both emerged with higher volumes and more efficient operations.

External initiatives are directed towards new opportunities in the local marketplace, and as such require a very different set of strategies from those that are internally focused. The first key success factor is simply the identification of a potentially viable opportunity, that is, one that is 'do-able' and consistent with the corporation's strategic priorities. Examples of this are the targeting of an energy management business by GE Canada in 1991, and the case of Pharma UK's transdermal technology development discussed in Chapter 3.

The second key factor for external initiatives is a relatively high degree of autonomy in the subsidiary. Faced with the strong likelihood of rejection if the project were presented to HQ management in its embryonic form, subsidiary managers typically prefer to do the initial development work with their own funds. Hewlett-Packard (Canada), for example, had access to development funds for country-specific projects during the 1980s, which facilitated the X-terminal development as well as several other projects. On the other hand, many subsidiaries do not have this level of autonomy. Some are able to assemble 'skunkworks' groups working in their own time to demonstrate the viability of their ideas. Others can not gain access to development funds, with the result that their promising ideas languish.

The third important factor concerns the tactics pursued by the initiative 'champion'. The champion always emerges in the early stages of the initiative – he or she is typically the individual who identifies the business opportunity in the first place, though sometimes the subsidiary general manager takes ownership of the project because of its importance to the subsidiary. A surprisingly consistent strategy is adopted by these individuals. First, the idea is tested in a small way, using subsidiary resources and without the knowledge of HQ. As the project takes shape, the initiative champion seeks out allies: typically local customers who are interested in buying the product or service, but sometimes also personal contacts or mentors at HQ. Finally, once the viability of the project has been demonstrated, the champion makes a formal representation to the HQ management and requests their investment and support. The HP (Canada) development project in Calgary led by Gerhard Schmid is an example of this. For seven years the group existed as an 'orphan' business without a line of reporting through one of HP's business groups. In 1992 the group finally achieved corporate legitimacy when it became a business unit within the test and measurement division.

While the internal and external initiative strategies appear very different, they do have their commonalities. First, they are both concerned with identifying the right opportunity to pursue. One subsidiary management team, for example, spent a decade unsuccessfully pursuing a 'big hit' investment before turning to a host of smaller projects that were much more successful. Second, they both involve identifying the major areas of resistance and finding ways of circumventing them. If the initiative threatens to put some people out of a job, for example, subsidiary managers should look for some form of compromise that can be interpreted as a win-win. Or if none of the HQ managers are known to them personally, they should try to involve someone with whom they have already developed a relationship. Finally, an important common theme is the need to couch the argument in objective rather than nationalistic arguments. As one manager put it, 'if I go down there wrapped in my Canadian flag, I provoke all sorts of unnecessary challenges'. Rather the imperative is to focus on technical or economic arguments about why the location makes sense.

Subsidiary strategy over the longer term

So much for the ways of getting a single initiative accepted. But what about the higher-order challenge of building a subsidiary strategy that makes sense in the medium or long term? The most insightful comment in this regard is that subsidiary activities should be thought of as peninsulas rather than islands. In other words, when the head office management look at what the subsidiary is doing, they should see it as a logical extension of their own core portfolio of activities, not as a stand-alone operation. If it turns out that the subsidiary has built an 'island' the consequences are likely to be bleak: lack of resources, because the activity is not strategic; or the possibility of closure or sell-off. Unfortunately it is also possible for the subsidiary to err too far the other way and build an activity that is so close to one being pursued at head office that it is not perceived as adding any value. In other words, the subsidiary management's longer-term strategy, and the one that should guide their specific initiatives, needs to be a delicate balancing act that combines uniqueness with relatedness. To some degree this balance can be shaped by head office managers, but experience suggests that it becomes much more coherent – and ultimately much more valuable – if it is steered through the visions and plans of the subsidiary management.

Thoughts for the HQ manager

If all these ideas about subsidiary initiative are to be effective, however, there has to be a corresponding shift in roles among HQ managers, essentially towards becoming more open to new and challenging ideas from the peripheral parts of the organization. This does not mean abandoning the tried and tested systems by which new proposals are evaluated, but it does require a change in attitude that will encourage more subsidiary managers to present their initiatives for consideration. A few key observations can be made.

First, systems can be instituted that encourage the flow of initiatives in a controlled manner. Some corporations send out 'request for proposal' invitations whenever major capital investments are planned; others have instituted 'challenge' mechanisms for changing internal sourcing relationships. These are organizational solutions and can be effective as a means of legitimizing subsidiary initiative. But they are not enough on their own.

Thus the second approach is for the top management to build systems that foster a cultural shift among HQ managers towards a more open-minded, geocentric view of the world. For example, several corporations use global business teams, secondments and transfers of senior managers as ways of breaking down narrow-minded prejudices and ethnocentric perspectives. Many also make a point of managing business units outside the home country, to reinforce the notion that ideas and opportunities in the peripheral parts of the organization matter.

Finally, in terms of managing the initiative process itself, it is important for the HQ management to be clear about the difference between challenging and resisting an initiative. A challenge is a means of seeking additional information, looking at alternatives and coming to a decision about the initiative's merits. Resistance involves many of the same techniques, but it is fundamentally prejudiced so it attaches greater importance to negative evidence. Many corporations have moved a long way towards challenging rather than resisting, but more needs to be done.

An important point to emphasize in this discussion is that the relationship between subsidiary and parent management needs to change, which involves adjustment on both sides. And unfortunately, in cases of mutual adjustment there is inevitably going to be some friction as both sides get used to the new arrangement. This issue is addressed next.

Evolution of the HQ–subsidiary relationship

The relationship between the HQ and subsidiary managers is clearly a complex one. To help make sense of it, at least with regard to the different attitudes towards initiative, a possible framework is presented in Figure 9.1. It suggests that at any point in time the subsidiary management can have a passive or an entrepreneurial approach to their role, while the HQ management can be closed or open to initiatives. Of course this is a gross simplification, but it represents a useful starting point for understanding how the relationship evolves. Four generic situations are suggested in Figure 9.1, as follows.

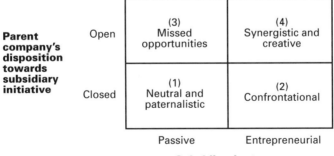

Figure 9.1 *Possible forms of HQ–subsidiary relationship*

Situation 1: where HQ managers are closed to initiative and the subsidiary's stance is passive, the relationship can be described as paternalistic. Alpha Corporation, the German manafacturer of plastic products mentioned in Chapter 2, exhibited this arrangement. The UK subsidiary was primarily a sales and marketing outlet for German-designed products. When questioned on the notion that the UK subsidiary might be in a position to identify and pursue new products or markets, the marketing manager's perspective was that there was no point because 'Someone in Germany would have already thought of it if it had any potential'. To the extent that there had to be *some* opportunities for market or product development in the UK, this statement essentially meant that 'Head office is not interested in pursuing opportunities that do not come from Germany'. His passive stance was, in other words, a learned response to the parent company's negative attitude. The relationship was 'harmonious' in that there was a common understanding of the subsidiary's role, but the implication is that the global reach of the corporation could end up being constrained by the lack of subsidiary initiatives.

Situation 2: where HQ managers are closed to initiative but the subsidiary is entrepreneurial the relationship is confrontational. The relationship between Pharma, a German pharmaceuticals company and its UK subsidiary, as described in Chapter 3, is typical in this regard. The UK subsidiary's attempts at initiative were repeatedly stonewalled by the major development group at head office, a process that was 'exhausting and frustrating' for both sides. The parent company was closed to initiatives, but in this case the subsidiary was convinced that it had developed an important product and was prepared to go to great lengths to have it approved. Only the recent formation of a country-neutral European marketing board allowed the UK management to circumvent the intransigence of the central R&D group.

Situation 3: a passive subsidiary coupled with HQ managers who are open to subsidiary initiative could best be characterized by 'missed opportunities'. While the first two scenarios could also lead to missed opportunities (in the eyes of a neutral observer), this is the only situation in which the absence of subsidiary initiative is evident to the parent company. An example of this was the Canadian Subsidiary of Gamma, a large US multinational. Gamma operated in a turbulent business environment where new business opportunities were plentiful. One middle manager pointed to a number of opportunities that he and others had spotted, and which he believed could lead to significant product innovations for the corporation as a whole. Unfortunately the senior management in Canada were focused on trying to turn the business around, and were interested only in projects with immediate financial returns. Several interesting projects were thus passed by, not because the parent company was closed to initiatives, but because the Canadian management were not prepared to take the lead.

Situation 4: finally, in the situation where the subsidiary is entrepreneurial and HQ managers are open to initiative, the relationship is synergistic. Many of the examples quoted in this book, including those of 3M Canada, Monsanto Canada and NCR Scotland, fit this description. It is the most effective arrangement because the latent potential within the national subsidiary is being exploited. For this arrangement to come about, however, both subsidiary and corporate managers must embrace their new roles, as described in this chapter.

More than just indicating the four possible scenarios, Figure 9.1 sheds some light on the dynamics of the HQ–subsidiary relationship. Quadrants 1 and 4 represent a level of balance between subsidiary stance and parent company disposition, which is a common understanding of the subsidiary's role in the corporation. Quadrants 2 and 3, by contrast, are indicative of disharmony, meaning that the two parties have different perspectives on the subsidiary's role. Intuitively, the disharmonious quadrants are liable to be transitional states. Over time either parent or subsidiary will shift its stance so that it falls into line with the stance of the other party. Thus a confrontational relationship will eventually lead to the subsidiary admitting defeat (and not pursuing further initiatives) or the parent company acknowledging the subsidiary's capabilities and allowing it greater discretion. Equally, the missed opportunities relationship will either cause the parent company to reverse its openness to subsidiary initiatives (on the assumption that the subsidiary has no entrepreneurial capability) or it will encourage the subsidiary to become entrepreneurial.

A further insight that can be gained from this framework is that the shift from quadrant 1 (paternalistic) to quadrant 4 (synergistic) must typically occur via quadrant 2 or 3, because it is very unlikely that the parent company and subsidiary will change simultaneously. Thus a confrontational relationship may seem to be frustrating, but it may be an important staging post on the way to a synergistic and creative relationship, assuming the parent company reacts favourably to the subsidiary's overtures. Equally a status of 'missed opportunities' may in fact represent the parent company trying to induce the subsidiary to become more entrepreneurial. In one case, for example, a new business manager in the US parent company was far more open than his predecessor to subsidiaries taking international responsibilities. His positive disposition was capitalized on by Canadian subsidiary managers, who were quickly able to convince him that they should be granted the world mandate for a major product line.

The costs of subsidiary initiative

Finally, it is important to return to the issue raised initially in Chapter 1, namely that subsidiary initiative does not occur without cost. As stressed in several places, many managers remain suspicious of subsidiary initiative, and of corporate entrepreneurship in general. They are suspicious in the first instance because it sounds like an oxymoron: perhaps an attractive idea in principle, but something that just does not happen very often. But the second reason for suspicion, and the one to be addressed in this section, is that subsidiary initiative has significant and often hidden costs. Initiative is, most of us would agree, an important engine of growth and renewal, whether it occurs inside the firm or in the economy as a whole. But as with most things, it is possible to have too much initiative. Listed below are four of the principal costs of subsidiary initiative of which managers need to be cognizant, and a number of suggestions about how those costs can be managed.

Empire building

We are all familiar with the stories. The country manager in France, for example, convinces head office that he needs to build a local manufacturing operation to keep the government happy. A few years later he comes out with some product changes that are 'essential to our continued success in France' but which cut against the worldwide positioning of the product. He then argues that a larger development team is needed to support the new product line because the R&D people back at head office do not understand the changes that have been made. And so on.

Is the country manager in France cleverly adapting the product to the unique French marketplace, or is he an empire builder, interested only in building his own power base at the expense of the firm? Similarly, if we take the Datacom Sweden manager or the US subsidiary manager of Alpha mentioned earlier, where do their priorities lie? The answer to these questions depends essentially on the preconceptions of the head office management. One preconception is that subsidiary managers are prone to act opportunistically and build their own little empires. The other is that the subsidiary management can be trusted and will act in the best interests of the corporation. The reality is that the 'facts' of the specific case can be interpreted to fit the manager's preconceptions. Obviously in a few cases there is solid evidence that the subsidiary's actions are either well-intentioned or oriented towards empire building, but most cases fall into the grey area where opinion is what matters.

So what can be done to guard against empire building? As a first objective, the head office–subsidiary relationship has to be built on trust, otherwise the strict control systems that ensue will make opportunistic behaviour a self-fulfilling prophecy. However that trust-based relationship must also be tempered by a system for evaluating and monitoring the subsidiary's initiatives to ensure that they are consistent with corporate goals. And it also needs to be undergirded and reinforced by a strong corporate culture that allows head office managers to be confident about the abilities and objectives of the subsidiary managers.

Lack of focus

This problem is related to empire building in that it is also the result of too much corporate entrepreneurship. Imagine that all employees take the idea of corporate entrepreneurship to heart and follow up their new ideas. Soon the firm is entering new businesses in every conceivable direction, with the result that financial resources are stretched too thinly and there is no coherence to the firm's product line. Hewlett Packard reportedly found itself in this position in the late 1980s because it had actively encouraged individual initiative but had not put in place the necessary controls. Changes were made to reduce the autonomy of subsidiary managers, but inevitably this approach also choked off the flow of initiatives, with the result that the company probably moved too far the other way.

Continuing to promote corporate entrepreneurship while not suffering from a lack of focus is a tricky balancing act. 3M is famous for managing this well – its approach is to 'let a thousand flowers bloom' in the early stages, but then quickly separate out and push forward the promising initiatives while weeding out the remainder. Such an approach needs careful management (see next section) and an organizational culture that rewards risk taking. It also has to embrace the idea that many good ideas will end up being pursued outside the firm. Ethicon, Johnson & Johnson's Scottish subsidiary, is a good example of this: it has on numerous occasions spun off businesses that did not fit its strategy, several of which have gone on to become major firms in their own right.

Costs of administering the internal market

Unlike the market economy, which appears to work best when left alone, the internal market system needs a considerable amount of administration to work effectively. One set of administrative costs result from setting up and maintaining the internal market system, for example defining the conditions under which sourcing relationships can be challenged and setting rules for transfer prices. There are also transaction costs that are accrued by the participating units every time an initiative is undertaken. Such costs are not only higher than would be the case in a centrally planned organization, they are also potentially higher than in an external market. In one case, for example, the head office management decided against sending out a 'request for proposal' to subsidiary companies because they did not want to spend the time going through all the proposals and justifying their decision to each subsidiary in turn. They chose instead to create their own shortlist of two or three subsidiaries, and evaluate them in detail.

As with the last point, there is a tricky balance here between maximizing the level of subsidiary initiative and keeping the cost of managing it under control. If head office managers draw up their own shortlist of subsidiaries, they keep the process under control but they may send the wrong signals to other entrepreneurially minded subsidiary managers. Again the rule of thumb appears to be one of keeping a very broad perspective at first, but fairly quickly weeding out those initiatives that are uncompetitive or do not align with the firm's needs.

Coping with 'internal unemployment'

The final cost of corporate entrepreneurship is that it can result in unemployment, either literally or figuratively. If we think about the market economy for a second, it is generally accepted that closing an inefficient coal mine is good for the economy as a whole but results in hundreds of layoffs in the old coal town. The same can be argued for the internal marketplace. If we consider the Honeywell case discussed earlier, the decision to move a production line from Minneapolis to Toronto was good for Honeywell as a whole (because it resulted in more efficient production) but it resulted in the loss of some jobs in Minneapolis. Such cases involve certain costs for the firm. Either the employees in question are laid off, which results in a one-off cost to the firm but, more importantly, the loss of some well-trained, experienced people, or they are retained by the firm and assigned new responsibilities, a process that inevitably takes time.

Of course the cost of closing down factories and reallocating people can be faced by all firms, but the point to emphasize here is that a system which encourages the use of an internal market will experience much more frequent changes in the allocation of activities to operating units, and will therefore suffer from a higher level of 'internal unemployment'. Just as the central planning system in Russia was able to boast of full employment until it all fell apart, centrally planned firms can keep the number of unassigned workers to a minimum for a long time, and then pay the price later through massive job losses. The costs of internal unemployment, in other words, are quite substantial, but probably worth paying because they are better than the alternative. The managerial challenge then becomes one of managing the reassigment of employees to other parts of the firm, and training them so that their skills match future needs.

Concluding comments

This completes the discussion of the managerial implications of the research. To some degree the suggestions are very specific, especially when they pertain to initiative strategies. But at the same time the observations are entirely consistent with much of the contemporary thinking on organizations. Bartlett and Ghoshal (1989), for example, advocate a shift towards a 'transnational' mind-set in large multinational corporations, which among other things involves a change in HQ–subsidiary roles from dependence to interdependence. Equally, much of the contemporary research on corporate entrepreneurship (for example Kanter, 1985) advocates greater entrepreneurial effort from below coupled with structural and cultural changes at the top. The findings in this study, then, echo much that has gone before, but with nuances and specific suggestions that are unique to the context of the study. And perhaps more importantly, with a relative emphasis on the perspective of the subsidiary manager, not the guys sitting in head office.

Key ideas in Chapter 9

- This chapter has provided some practical advice on encouraging subsidiary initiative. For subsidiary managers, the best advice is to tailor your initiative strategy to the existing skills of the subsidiary and the openness of HQ managers. Start small, and build allies along the way both with decision makers at HQ and with external partners such as lead customers. Depending on your degree of freedom, a skunkworks-type approach may be valid, but even here it is important to stay close to the strategic priorities of the parent company.
- For HQ managers, it is important to look at the MNC as a whole in order to understand the ways that subsidiary initiatives are funded and the ways in which they can be shot down. The challenge is to build a system with sufficient 'slack' that initiatives are brought to the surface (different funding mechanisms, some local autonomy), while retaining enough control to ensure that the less-attractive ideas do not find their way through.
- A major part of the challenge in encouraging subsidiary initiative is to understand the existing relationship between subsidiary and HQ. Ideally their mind-sets are aligned, so that initiative from the subsidiary is met with openness by the HQ. But if the subsidiary's initiative-taking stance is countered by a closed-minded HQ attitude, a confrontational relationship will emerge. This is a common scenario that requires discussion and typically some level of compromise to be resolved.
- There is a dark side to subsidiary initiative that has been largely set to one side in this book. Some managers pursue initiative purely for their own empire-building ends. It is also possible that too many initiatives will result in a lack of strategic focus in the MNC. These and other negatives were discussed in the final section of this chapter, and advice was given on how to minimize the downside of subsidiary initiative.

Appendix: A Note on the Research Methodology

This book is based on approximately five years of research, some of which was extremely unstructured (open-ended interviews) and some very carefully designed (development and administration of a questionnaire). This appendix provides a fairly short description of the various phases of the research programme and the methodologies used in each phase. If any readers are interested in the finer points of the methodology, they should consult some of the scholarly articles that I have published from the research (e.g. Birkinshaw 1996, 1997).

Phase 1: exploration and identification of the research phenomenon

In the summer of 1992 I first began looking into foreign-owned subsidiary companies in Canada. I was still in the early stage of my doctoral studies and I was looking for an appropriate thesis topic. Nick Fry, who later became my thesis supervisor, suggested that I look into country management in foreign subsidiaries 'because there is a lot happening there'. With the help of various leads I began a round of informal interviews in prominent Canadian subsidiary companies, such as GE Canada, Du Pont Canada and 3M Canada. While country management was clearly an issue in these companies, it became apparent to me that the main concern of country managements – regardless of how big or small – was their ability to attract or retain investment in the wake of the recently signed Free Trade Agreement. This led me to focus on the emergence of 'world mandate' activities in Canadian subsidiaries as a response to the threat (or opportunity) of free trade, a subject with a lot of prior research and a considerable amount of political baggage attached to it.

In pushing further on the world mandate phenomenon, however, I became far more fascinated with the *process* than the end result, because it seemed that the process was what subsidiary managements were really concerned with. More interviews followed, mostly of the semistructured variety, and I also became involved in a variety of industrial and governmental initiatives (for example the Conference Board of Canada, the Electrical Manufacturers Association, the Ontario Government) that were looking into these issues at the same time.

My doctoral thesis proposal, defended in autumn 1993, focused on a messy combination of the end result (the mandate) and the process (the subsidiary initiative), with a variety of academic theories ranging from corporate entrepreneurship to agency theory to support my ideas. While only half-baked at this stage, my ideas were far enough along that I was given the go-ahead to pursue them through a fairly structured set of interviews in six subsidiaries.

Phase 2: structured clinical research in six subsidiaries

My doctoral thesis ended up consisting of data on about 39 initiatives in six Canadian subsidiaries – 3M, Monsanto, Hewlett-Packard, Honeywell Homes division, Honeywell Buildings division and Amazon (the latter a disguised name). These six companies were identified and approached in autumn 1993 and spring 1994, and the research was conducted throughout 1994. In total I conducted exactly 100 interviews of around one hour each.

My goal in each of these six companies was to investigate all their significant initiatives. *A priori* it was impossible to know what to expect, so I adopted a very broad definition of 'initiative' (something entrepreneurial that leads to some sort of mandate in the subsidiary) and pursued all avenues. I ended up with 39 initiatives, or between three and 10 per company. Some of these were very old, having taken place in the 1960s, but most had occurred during the previous 10 years. I typically interviewed several people about each initiative in order to obtain contrasting perspectives, and in around half the cases I got someone from head office in the US to give me their account of what had happened.

The final sample was not comprehensive, but it was pretty close. I know I missed a few small initiatives in 3M, and I am certain that some failed initiatives had occurred but were not made known to me. The shortage of failures, in fact, was an obvious weakness in my research. Not a fatal flaw, in that I was more interested in the process than an explanation of success *per se*, but one which I think needs addressing in the future.

Data was collected through semistructured interviews, all of which were taped and subsequently transcribed. In addition, towards the end of the research I sent around a short questionnaire that was directed towards the key individual (the 'champion') in each initiative. This data allowed me to obtain some objective verification of my subjective findings.

I conducted the data analysis and wrote up my doctoral thesis in the latter half of 1994. Analysis of interview data is a messy process at the best of times, but through the careful use of tables and graphs I was able to structure my thinking and eventually put together an informative typology of subsidiary initiatives (cf. Miles and Huberman, 1984). This typology proved to be something of a breakthrough, because it allowed me to tie iniatives to the network theory of the MNC (see Chapter 2), and also to lay out the various processes that had occurred in each case. The subsequent ideas on the corporate immune system (Chapter 3) and subsidiary development (Chapter 4) built on this typology.

My doctoral thesis was completed in December 1994 and defended in May 1995. While many of my ideas had moved on and I had already begun collecting some follow-up data, I made the pragmatic decision to limit the thesis to the 39 initiatives in six Canadian subsidiaries.

Phase 3: clinical research in other settings

One concern that emerged during my doctoral work was that I was looking at a Canadian phenomenon, that is, something that had limited applicability to other settings. Because of this I kept my antennae up in the hope of coming across similar phenomena in different countries. One such case was Pharma AG (not its real name), a German pharmaceuticals company and its British subsidiary. This is mentioned several times in the book because it is a fascinating example of subsidiary initiative and the problems thereof. Another set of cases presented themselves to me in Scotland through my contacts with Professors Neil Hood and Steve Young at Strathclyde University, with the result that I spent three months in the summer of 1995 located there, conducting interviews at NCR, IBM and other interesting companies. Finally, I conducted a small number of interviews in Sweden when I first moved there in autumn 1995, again focused on cases of subsidiary initiative. These interviews were undertaken with Karl Källén, a masters student.

The purpose of all these additional interviews was what Yin (1984) would call theoretical replication, examining the same basic phenomenon of subsidiary initiative but in different settings that would be expected to yield somewhat different findings. And indeed, what I uncovered was a variant of the original theme – much more focus on big manufacturing investments in Scotland, with a significant host-country attraction component, and a centre-of-excellence model in Sweden involving very little in the way of new investment but quite a lot of intangible knowledge flows.

Using the theoretical replication logic, my current research could also be seen as falling within this project, because I am now focusing on the perspective of head office managers on various subsidiary-level actions and activities. This allows me to some degree to test the hypothesis that subsidiary initiative varies not just by company but also by country.

Phase 4: large sample questionnaire study

The final stage of my research programme, which also overlapped phase 3 to some extent, was a questionnaire administered to a sample of subsidiaries in Canada, Scotland and Sweden. This project began while I was still in Canada and was the logical conclusion to my doctoral thesis (even though I decided not to include it). The questionnaire was directed to the presidents of subsidiary companies and asked about the subsidiary, its capabilities, its relationship with head office, its local market environment and any evidence of initiatives. Thus it sought to find out two things: (1) why certain subsidiaries appeared to be initiative takers while others were not, and (2) what factors predicted different types of initiative. A total of 81 Canadian subsidiaries responded to the questionnaire. Subsequently I administered a version of it in Scotland, with Neil Hood's help, and one in Sweden, with help from Stefan Jonsson. The final tally was 229 valid questionnaire responses in the three countries. The findings in Chapters 4 and 5, in particular, draw heavily from this database, and it has spawned a number of other papers as well.

Phase 5: ongoing investigation into large MNCs

While the formal investigation of subsidiary initiative can be said to have finished in 1996 my interest in the issue continues, and as a result of my ongoing research in related areas new examples and new insights emerge all the time. To be more specific, I am just concluding a detailed examination of the network organizations of five large Swedish MNCs, and some of the ideas emerging from that study have inevitably found their way into this book. Chapter 8, in which I describe the internal market model, has been particularly influenced by this current research.

References

Amit, R. and Schoemaker, P. (1993) 'Strategic assets and organizational rent', *Strategic Management Journal*, 14: 33–46.

Arthur, B. (1996) 'Increasing returns and the new world of business', *Harvard Business Review*, 74 (3): 100–12.

Arvidsson, N. (1999) 'The ignorant MNE: The role of perception gaps in knowledge management', doctoral dissertation, Stockholm School of Economics.

Barnard, Chester I. (1938) *The Functions of the Executive*. Cambridge, MA: Harvard University Press.

Barnes, J. (1984) Cognitive biases and their impact on strategic planning', *Strategic Management Journal*, 5: 129–38.

Barney, Jay (1991) 'Firm resources and sustained competitive advantage', *Journal of Management*, 17 (1): 99–120.

Bartlett, C.A. (1979) 'Multinational structural evolution: The changing decision environment in international divisions', unpublished doctoral dissertation, Harvard University.

Bartlett, Christopher A. and Ghoshal, Sumantra (1986) 'Tap your subsidiaries for global reach', *Harvard Business Review*, 64 (6): 87–94.

Bartlett, Christopher A. and Ghoshal, Sumantra (1989) *Managing across Borders: The Transnational Solution*. Boston: Harvard Business School Press.

Bartlett, Christopher A. and Ghoshal, Sumantra (1993) 'Beyond the M-Form: Toward a managerial theory of the firm', *Strategic Management Journal*, 14: 23–46.

Bartlett, Christopher A. and Ghoshal, Sumantra (1995) 'Rebuilding behavioural context: Turn process reengineering into people revitalization', *Sloan Management Review*, Fall: 11–23.

Baumol, W.J. (1968) 'Entrepreneurship in economic theory', *American Economic Review* (papers and proceedings), 58: 65–71.

Birkinshaw, Julian M. (1995) 'Entrepreneurship in multinational corporations: The initiative process in foreign subsidiaries', unpublished doctoral disseration, Westen Business School, University of Western Ontario.

Birkinshaw, J.M. (1996) 'How subsidiary mandates are gained and lost', *Journal of International Business Studies*, 27 (3): 467–96.

Birkinshaw, J.M. (1997) 'Entrepreneurship in multinational corporations: The characteristics of subsidiary initiatives', *Strategic Management Journal*, 18 (2): 207–30.

Bower, Joseph L. (1970) *Managing the Resource Allocation Process: A Study of Corporate Planning and Investment*. Boston, MA: Harvard Business School Press.

Brandt, W.K. and Hulbert, J.M. (1977) 'Headquarters guidance in marketing strategy in the multinational subsidiary', *Columbia Journal of World Business*, 12 (Winter): 7–14.

Buckley, P.J. and Casson, M.C. (1976) *The Future of the Multinational Enterprise*. London: MacMillan.

Burgelman, Robert A. (1983a) 'A process model of internal corporate venturing in the diversified major firm', *Administrative Science Quarterly*, 28: 223–44.

Burgelman, Robert A. (1983b) 'A model of the interaction of strategic behavior, corporate context and the concept of strategy', *Academy of Management Review*, 8 (1): 61–70.

Burgelman, Robert A. (1983c) 'Corporate entrepreneurship and strategic management: insights from a process study', *Management Science*, 29 (12): 1349–63.

Burgelman, Robert A. (1991) 'Intraorganizational ecology of strategy making and organizational adaptation: Theory and field research', *Organization Science*, 2(3): 239–62.

Burns, Thomas J. and Stalker, G. (1961) *The Management of Innovation*. London: Tavistock.

Cantillon, R. (1755) 'The circulation and exchange of goods and merchandise' in H. Higgs (ed.), *Essai sur la Nature du Commerce en General*. London: MacMillan, 1931.

Casson, Mark C. (1990) *Entrepreneurship*. Aldershot: Edward Elgar.

Chandler, A.D. (1962) *Strategy and Structure: Chapters in the History of the American Industrial Enterprise*. Cambridge, MA: MIT Press.

Cohen, Michael D., March, James G. and Olsen, John P. (1972) 'A garbage can model of organizational choice', *Administrative Science Quarterly*, 17: 1–25.

Connor, K. (1991) 'A historical comparison of resource based theory and five schools within industrial organization economics: Do we have a new theory of the firm?', *Journal of Management*, 17(1): 121–54.

Covin, J.G. and Slevin, D.P. (1991) 'A conceptual model of entrepreneurship as firm behavior', *Entrepreneurship Theory and Practice*, Fall: 7–25.

Cray, David (1984) 'Control and coordination in multinational corporations', *Journal of International Business Studies*, 15 (3): 85–98.

Crookell, Harold H. (1986) 'Specialization and international competitiveness', in Hamid Etemad and Louis Seguin Dulude (eds), *Managing the Multinational Subsidiary*. London: Croom Helm, pp. 102–11.

Crookell, Harold H. (1990) *Canadian–American Trade and Investment under the Free Trade Agreement*. New York: Quorum Books.

Damanpour, Faramarz (1991) 'Organizational innovation: A meta-analysis of effects of determinants and moderators', *Academy of Management Journal*, 34: 555–90.

Daniels, John D., Pitts, Robert A. and Tretter, Maryann J. (1984) 'Strategy and structure of U.S. multinationals: an exploratory study', *Academy of Management Journal*, 27 (2): 292–307.

Day, Diana (1994) 'Raising radicals: Different processes for championing innovative corporate ventures', *Organization Science*, 5 (2): 148–72.

D'Cruz, Joseph R. (1986) 'Strategic management of subsidiaries', in Hamid Etemad and Louis Seguin Dulude (eds), *Managing the Multinational Subsidiary*. London: Croom Helm, pp. 75–89.

Dierickx, I. and Cool, K. (1989) 'Asset stock accumulation and sustainability of competitive advantage', *Management Science*, 35 (12): 1504–13.

Dougherty, Deborah (1992) 'Interpretive barriers to successful product innovation in large firms', *Organization Science*, 3 (2): 179–202.

Dougherty, Deborah and Heller, T. (1994) 'The illegitimacy of successful product innovation in established firms', *Organization Science*, 5 (2): 200–18.

Doz, Yves L. (1976) 'National policies and multinational management', unpublished doctoral dissertation, Harvard Business School, Boston.

Dunning, John H. (1980) 'Towards an eclectic theory of international production; some empirical tests', *Journal of International Business Studies*, 11: 9–31.

Dunning, J.H. (1988) 'The eclectic paradigm of international production: A restatement and some possible extensions', *Journal of International Business Studies*, Spring: 1–31.

Dunning, J.H. (1993) *Multinational Enterprises and the Global Economy.* Wokingham: Addison-Wesley.

Eccles, R. (1985) *The Transfer Pricing Problem: A Theory for Practise.* Lexington, MA: D.C. Heath.

Egelhoff, William G. (1982) 'Strategy and structure in multinational corporations: An information-processing view', *Administrative Science Quarterly*, 27: 435–58.

Emerson, R.M. (1962) 'Power-dependence relations', *American Sociological Review*, 27: 31–41.

Etemad, Hamid and Dulude, Louis Seguin (1986) *Managing the Multinational Subsidiary.* London: Croom Helm.

Fayerweather, John (1969) *International Business Strategy and Administration.* Cambridge, MA: Ballinger.

Fayerweather, J. (1982) *Host National Attitudes towards Multinational Corporations.* New York: Praeger.

Forsgren, Mats and Johanson, Jan (1992) *Managing Networks in International Business.* Philadelphia: Gordon & Breach.

Franko, Lawrence (1974) 'The move toward a multidivisional structure in European organizations', *Administrative Science Quarterly*, 19: 493–506.

Gage Canadian Dictionary (1983) Toronto: Gage Educational.

Galbraith, Jay (1982) 'Designing the innovating organization', *Organizational Dynamics*, Winter: 5–25.

Galunic, D. Charles (1996) 'Recreating divisional domains: Intracorporate evolution and the multibusiness firm', in J.B. Keys and L.N. Dosier (eds), *Proceedings of the Academy of Management Annual Meeting.* Madison, WI: Omnipress.

Galunic, D.C. and Eisenhardt, K.M. (1996) The evolution of intracorporate domains: Divisional charter losses in high-technology, multidivisional corporations', *Organization Science*, 7 (3): 255–81.

Gates, Stephen R. and Egelhoff, William G. (1986) 'Centralization in headquarters–subsidiary relationships', *Journal of International Business Studies*, 17 (2): 71–92.

Ghoshal, Sumantra (1986) 'The innovative multinational: A differentiated network of organizational roles and management processes', unpublished doctoral dissertation, Harvard Business School, Boston.

Ghoshal, Sumantra and Bartlett, Christopher A. (1988) 'Creation, adoption and diffusion of innovations by subsidiaries of multinational corporations', *Journal of International Business Studies*, 19 (3): 365–88.

Ghoshal, Sumantra and Bartlett, Christopher A. (1990) 'The multinational corporation as an interorganizational network', *Academy of Management Review*, 15 (4): 603–25.

Ghoshal, Sumantra and Bartlett, Christopher A. (1994) 'Linking organizational context and managerial action: The dimensions of quality of management', *Strategic Management Journal*, 15: 91–112.

Ghoshal, S. and Moran, P. (1996) 'Bad for practice: A critique of the transaction cost theory', *Academy of Management Review*. 21: 13–47.

Ghoshal, Sumantra and Nohria, Nitin (1989) 'Internal differentiation within multinational corporations', *Strategic Management Journal*, 10: 323–37.

Ginsberg, Ari and Hay, Michael (1995) 'Confronting the challenges of corporate entrepreneurship: Guidelines for venture managers', *European Management Journal*, 12 (4): 382–9.

Grant, R. (1998) *Contemporary Strategy Analysis*. Oxford: Blackwell.

Greenfield, Liah (1994) *Nationalism*. Cambridge, MA: Harvard University Press.

Gupta, Anil K. and Govindarajan, Vijay (1991) 'Knowledge flows and the structure of control within multinational corporations', *Academy of Management Review*, 16 (4): 768–92.

Halal, W. (1994) 'From hierarchy to enterprise: Internal markets are the new foundation of management', *Academy of Management Executive*, 8 (4): 69–83.

Halal, W.E., Geranmayeh, A. and Pourdehnad, J. (1993) *Internal Markets: Bringing the Power of Free Enterprise Inside your Organization*. New York: John Wiley.

Hamel, G. and Prahalad, C.K. (1985) 'Do you really have a global strategy?', *Harvard Business Review*, 63 (4): 139–45.

Hannan, M. and Freeman, J. (1977) 'The population ecology of organizations', *American Journal of Sociology*, 82: 929–64.

Hayek, F.A. (1937) 'Economics and knowledge', *Economica*, 3: 33–54.

Hedlund, Gunnar (1986) 'The hypermodern MNC: a heterarchy?', *Human Resource Management*, 25: 9–36.

Hedlund, Gunnar (1994) 'A model of knowledge management and the N-form corporation', *Strategic Management Journal*, 15: 73–90.

Hedlund, G. (1997) 'The MNC as a nearly recomposable system', paper presented at the Academy of International Business meeting, Banff, Canada.

Hedlund, Gunnar and Ridderstråle, Jonas (1997) 'Toward a theory of the self-renewing MNC', in B. Toyne and D. Nigh (eds), *International Business: An Emerging Vision*. Columbia, SC: University of South Carolina Press.

Hedlund, G. and Rolander, D. (1990) 'Action in heterarchies – new approaches to managing the MNC', in C.A. Bartlett, Y.L. Doz and G. Hedlund (eds), *Managing the Global Firm*. London: Routledge.

Hennart, J.F. (1991) 'Control in multinational firms: The role of price and hierarchy', *Management International Review*, 31 (special issue): 71–96.

Hennart, J.F. (1993) 'Explaining the swollen middle: Why most transactions are a mix of "market" and "hierarchy" ', *Organization Science*, 4 (4): 529–47.

Huber, G. (1991) 'Organizational learning: The contributing processes and the literatures', *Organization Science*, 2 (1): 88–115.

Hymer, Stephen (1960/1976) 'The international operations of national firms: a study of foreign direct investment'. PhD dissertation, Massachusetts Institute of Technology.

Imai, K., Nonaka, I. and Takeuchi, H. (1985) 'Managing the new product development process: How Japanese companies learn and unlearn', in K.B. Clark, R.H. Hayes and C. Lorenz (eds), *The Uneasy Alliance*. Cambridge, MA: Harvard Business School Press.

Jacobson, Robert (1992) 'The "Austrian" school of strategy', *Academy of Management Review*, 17 (4): 782–807.

Jarillo, Jose-Carlos and Martinez, Jon I. (1990) 'Different roles for subsidiaries: The case of multinational corporations', *Strategic Management Journal*, 11: 501–12.

Johanson, Jan and Vahlne, Jan-Erik (1977) 'The internationalization process of the firm – A model of knowledge development and increasing foreign market commitments', *Journal of International Business Studies*, 1: 23–32.

Kanter, Rosabeth M. (1982) 'The middle manager as innovator', *Harvard Business Review*, July–August: 95–105.

Kanter, Rosabeth M. (1985) *The Change Masters*. New York: Simon & Schuster.

Kanter, Rosabeth M. (1996) *World Class*. New York: Simon and Schuster.

Katz, Ralph and Allen, Thomas J. (1982) 'Investigating the not invented here syndrome: A look at the performance, tenure and communication patterns of 50 R&D project groups', *R&D Management*, 12 (1): 7–19.

Kidder, T. (1971) *The Soul of a New Machine*. Boston, MA: Little, Brown.

Kirzner, Israel M. (1973) *Competition and Entrepreneurship*. Chicago: University of Chicago Press.

Knight, Frank H. (1921) *Risk, Uncertainty and Profit*. Chicago: University of Chicago Press.

Kogut, B. (1985) 'Designing global strategies: Comparative and competitive value-added chains', *Sloan Management Review*, Summer: 15–27.

Kogut, Bruce and Zander, Udo (1992) 'Knowledge of the firm, combinative capabilities and the replication of technology', *Organisation Science*, 3 (3): 383–97.

Kogut, Bruce and Zander, Udo (1995) 'Knowledge of the firm and the evolutionary theory of the multinational corporation', *Journal of International Business Studies*, 25 (4): 625–46.

Kotter, John and Schlesinger, Leonard (1979) 'Choosing strategies for change', *Harvard Business Review*, March–April: 106–14.

Lawrence, Paul (1954) 'How to deal with resistance to change', *Harvard Business Review*, May–June: 49–56.

Lawrence, Paul and Lorsch, Jay (1967) *Organization and Environment: Managing Differentiation and Integration*. Boston, MA: Harvard University Press.

Leibenstein, H. (1966) 'Allocative efficiency vs. "X-Efficiency"', *American Economic Review*, June: 392–415.

Leibenstein, H. (1968) 'Entrepreneurship and development', in *Proceedings of the American Economic Association*, 72–83.

Madhok, Anoop (1997) 'Cost, value and foreign market entry mode: The transaction and the firm', *Strategic Management Journal*, 18: 39–61.

Malnight, T. (1994) 'Globalization of an ethnocentric firm: An evolutionary perspective', *Strategic Management Journal*, 16: 119–41.

Malnight, T. (1996) 'The transition from decentralized to network-based MNC structures: An evolutionary perspective', *Journal of International Business Studies*, 27 (1): 43–66.

March, James G. (1991) 'Exploration and exploitation in organizational learning', *Organization Science*, 2 (1): 71–87.

March, James G. and Simon, Herbert (1958) *Organizations*. New York: Wiley.

Martinez, Jon I. and Jarillo, J. Carlos (1989) 'The evolution of research on coordination mechanisms in multinational corporations', *Journal of International Business Studies*, Fall: 489–514.

Meyer, J.W. and Rowan, B. (1997) 'Institutionalized organizations: Formal structure as myth and ceremony', *American Journal of Sociology*, 83 (2): 340–63.

Miles, M.B. and Huberman, M. (1984) *Qualitative Data Analysis: A Sourcebook of New Methods*. Newbury Park, CA: Sage.

Miller, Danny (1983) 'The correlates of entrepreneurship in three types of firms', *Management Science*, 29: 770–91.

Mises, L. (1949) *Human Action: A Treatise on Economics*. New Haven, CT: Yale University Press.

Moore, Karl (1994) 'Capturing international responsibilities in the Canadian pharmaceutical industry', *Industry Canada Working Paper*. Ottawa: Industry Canada.

Moran, P. and Ghoshal, S. (1999) 'Markets, firms and the process of economic development', *Academy of Management Review*, 24 (3): 390–412.

Morgan, G. (1986) *Images of Organizations*. Thousand Oaks, CA: Sage.

Nelson, R. and Winter, S. (1982) *An Evolutionary Theory of Economic Change*. Cambridge, MA: Harvard University Press.

Nonaka, Ikujiro and Takeuchi, Hirotake (1995) *The Knowledge-Creating Company*. New York: Oxford University Press.

Otterbeck, Lars (ed.) (1981) *The Management of Headquarters–Subsidiary Relations in Multinational Corporations*. Hampshire: Gower.

Penrose, Edith T. (1959) *The Theory of the Growth of the Firm*. Oxford: Basil Blackwell.

Perlmutter, Howard V. (1969) 'The tortuous evolution of the multinational corporation', *Columbia Journal of World Business*, Jan–Feb: 9–18.

Pfeffer, J.R. and Salancik, G.R. (1978) *The External Control of Organisations*. New York: Harper and Row.

Pinchott, Gifford III (1985) *Intrapreneuring*. New York: Harper & Row.

Popper, K.R. (1968) *The Logic of Scientific Discovery*. New York: Harper and Row.

Porter, M.E. (1980) *Competitive Strategy*. New York: Free Press.

Porter, M.E. (1990) *The Competitive Advantage of Nations*. New York: Free Press.

Poynter, Thomas A. and Rugman, Alan M. (1982) 'World product mandates: How will multinationals respond?', *Business Quarterly*, Autumn: 54–61.

Prahalad, C.K. (1975) 'The strategic process in a multinational corporation', unpublished doctoral dissertation, School of Business Administration, Harvard University.

Prahalad, C.K. and Doz, Yves L. (1981) 'An approach to strategic control in MNCs', *Sloan Management Review*, Summer: 5–13.

Prahalad, C.K. and Doz, Yves L. (1987) *The Multinational Mission*. New York: Free Press.

Quinn, J.B. (1985) 'Managing innovation: Controlled chaos', *Harvard Business Review*, 63 (3): 73–84.

Ridderstråle, J. (1996) *Global Innovation.* Stockholm: Institute of International Business.

Rosenzweig, P. and Singh, J. (1991) 'Organizational environments and the multinational enterprise', *Academy of Management Review,* 16 (2): 340–61.

Rothwell, R. (1977) 'The characteristics of succesful innovators and technically progressive firms', *R&D Management,* 7 (3).

Rugman, Alan M. (1981) *Inside the Multinationals: The Economics of Internal Markets.* London: Croom Helm.

Rugman, A.M. (1983) *Multinationals and Technology Transfer.* New York: Praeger.

Rugman, A.M. and Bennett, J. (1982) 'Technology transfer and world product mandating in Canada', *Columbia Journal of World Business,* 17 (4): 58–62.

Rugman, A.M. and Douglas, S. (1986) 'The strategic management of multinationals and world product mandating', *Canadian Public Policy,* 12 (2): 320–8.

Rugman, Alan and Verbeke, Alain (1992) 'A note on the transnational solution and the transaction cost theory of multinational strategic management', *Journal of International Business Studies,* 23 (4): 761–72.

Safarian, A.E. (1966) *Foreign Ownership of Canadian Industry.* Toronto: McGraw-Hill.

Sathe, Vijay (1985) 'Managing an entrepreneurial dilemma: Nurturing entrepreneurship and control in large corporations', in J.A. Hornaday, E.B. Shils, J.A. Timmons, and K.H. Vesper (eds), *Frontiers of Entrepreneurship Research.* Wellesley, MA: Babson College, pp. 636–57.

Schollhammer, H. (1982) 'Internal corporate entrepreneurship', in D. Sexton and K.H. Vesper (eds), *Encyclopedia of Entrepreneurship.* Englewood Cliffs, NJ: Prentice-Hall, pp. 209–23.

Schön, Donald (1971) *Beyond the Stable State.* New York: Norton.

Schumpeter, Joseph A. (1934) *The Theory of Economic Development.* Cambridge, MA: Harvard University Press.

Schwenk, Charles (1988) 'The cognitive perspective on strategic decision making', *Journal of Management Studies,* 25 (1): 41–55.

Science Council of Canada (1980) *Multinationals and Industrial Strategy: The Role of World Product Mandates,* Science Council of Canada, Supply and Services Canada, Ottawa.

Sim, A.B. (1977) 'Decentralized management of subsidiaries and their performance', *Management International Review,* 2: 45–52.

Simon, Herbert (1957) *Models of Man.* New York: Wiley.

Simon, Herbert (1976) *Adminstrative Behaviour,* 4th edn. New York: Free Press.

Snow, C.C., Miles, R.E. and Coleman, H.J. (1992) 'Managing 21st century network organizations', *Organizational Dynamics,* Winter: 4–20.

Stevenson, Howard H. and Jarillo, Jose-Carlos (1990) 'A paradigm of entrepreneurship: Entrepreneurial management', *Strategic Management Journal,* 11: 17–27.

Stopford, John M. and Baden-Fuller, Charles W.F. (1994) 'Creating corporate entrepreneurship', *Strategic Management Journal,* 15: 521–36.

Stopford, John M. and Wells, Louis T. (1972) *Managing the Multinational Enterprise: Organisations of the Firm and Ownership of the Subsidiaries.* New York: Basic Books.

Sykes, Hollister B. (1986) 'The anatomy of a corporate venturing program: Factors influencing success', *Journal of Business Venturing*, 1: 275–93.

Szulanski, G. (1996) 'Exploring internal stickiness: Impediments to the transfer of best practises within the firm', *Strategic Management Journal*, 17 (special issue): 27–44.

Taggart, J.H. (1996) 'Multinational manufacturing subsidiaries in Scotland: Strategic role and economic impact', *International Business Review*, 5 (5): 447–68.

Taggart, J.H. (1997) 'Autonomy and procedural justice: A framework for evaluating subsidiary strategy', *Journal of International Business Studies*, 28 (1): 51–76.

Teece, D.J., Pisano, G. and Shuen, A. (1997) 'Dynamic capabilities and strategic management', *Strategic Management Journal*, 18: 509–34.

Tversky, A. and Kahneman, D. (1974) 'Judgement under uncertainty: Heuristics and biases', *Sciences*, 185: 1124–31.

Van de Ven, Andrew and Garud, Raghu (1995) 'The coevolution of technical and institutional events in the development of an innovation', in J. Baum and J. Singh (eds) *Evolutionary Dynamics of Organizations*. New York: Oxford University Press, pp. 425–43.

Vernon, Raymond (1966) 'International investment and international trade in the product cycle', *Quarterly Journal of Economics*, May: 191–207.

Vernon, Raymond (1979) 'The product cycle hypothesis in a new international environment', *Oxford Bulletin of Economics and Statistics*, 41: 255–67.

Watson, Tony J. (1982) 'Group ideologies and organizational change', *Journal of Management Studies*, 19 (3): 259–75.

Weick, Karl E. (1979) *The Social Psychology of Organizing*. Reading, MA: Addison-Wesley.

Weick, Karl E. (1987) 'Substitutes for corporate strategy', in D.J. Teece (ed.), *The Competitive Challenge*. New York: Harper & Row.

Wernerfelt, B. (1984) 'A resource based view of the firm', *Strategic Management Journal*, 5: 171–80.

Westney, D. Eleanor (1990) 'Internal and external linkages in the MNC: The case of R&D subsidiaries in Japan', in C.A. Bartlett, Y. Doz and G. Hedlund (eds), *Managing the Global Firm*. London: Routledge, pp. 279–302.

Westney, D. Eleanor (1994) 'Institutionalization theory and the multinational corporation', in S. Ghoshal and D.E. Westney (eds), *Organization Theory and the Multinational Corporation*. New York: St Martin's Press, pp. 53–76.

White, Roderick E. and Poynter, Thomas A. (1984) 'Strategies for foreign-owned subsidiaries in Canada', *Business Quarterly*, Summer: 59–69.

White, Roderick E. and Poynter, Thomas A. (1990) 'Achieving worldwide advantage with the horizontal organization', *Business Quarterly*, Autumn: 55–60.

Williamson, O.E. (1975) *Markets and Hierarchies: Analysis and Antitrust Implications*. New York: The Free Press.

Williamson, O.E. (1991) 'Comparative economic organization: The analysis of discrete structural alternatives', *Administrative Science Quarterly*, 36: 269–96.

Yin, R.K. (1984) *Case Study Research*. Beverly Hills, CA: Sage.

Zander, I. (1994) 'The tortoise evolution of the multinational corporation', doctoral dissertation, Institute of International Business, Stockholm School of Economics.

Zander, U. (1991) 'Exploiting a technological edge – Voluntary and involuntary dissemination of technology', doctoral dissertation, Stockholm School of Economics.

Index